Absolute Financial English

by Julie Pratten

DELTA Publishing
Quince Cottage
Hoe Lane
Peaslake
Surrey GU5 9SW
England

www.deltapublishing.co.uk

First published 2009
Reprinted 2010, 2012

Edited by Catriona Watson-Brown
Designed by Caroline Johnston
Cover design by Peter Bushell
Cartoons supplied by CartoonStock
Photos on page 76 by Corbis (right)
and iStock (left)
Audio production by Ian Harker
Printed in China by RR Donnelley

ISBN 978-1-905085-28-6

Acknowledgments

The author and publisher gratefully acknowledge the following for permission
to reproduce copyright material:

Page 13: adapted from *How a good balance sheet helped me to improve my business*,
http://rudi-riyanto.blogspot.com/2008_01_01_archive.html

Page 15: adapted from *It's time to tackle accountants' stereotypes* by Michael Snyder,
published in *Accountancy Age*, 27th September 2007

Page 23: adapted from *The changing face of accounting* by Anton B. Van Wyk and
David G. Taylor, reprinted with permission from December 2004 issue of *Internal
Auditor*, published by The Institute of Internal Auditors, Inc. www.theiia.org

Page 30: adapted from *Choosing the right software*, www.just-tax.co.uk/guide_as.htm

Page 32: adapted from *Choosing accounting software* by Steve Garrett,
Link Systems UK

Page 41: adapted from *Investors should look beyond BRIC countries, says PwC report*
by Jason Gorringe, Tax-News.com, 10th March 2008

Page 42: adapted and licensed under the GNU Free Documentation Licence from
Wikipedia information

Page 49: adapted from Adobe-Efrag-Zalm080318(1)pdf

Page 51: adapted from *Forensic accountant – detective, accountant, auditor or attorney?*
by Thomas Levanti, www.nysscpa.org/sound_advice/forensic_acc.htm

Page 58: adapted from *Why credit-rating agencies blew it: mystery solved*,
http://robertreich.blogspot.com/2007/10/they-mystery-of-why-credit-
rating.html

Pages 60–61: adapted from *Ethical reporting principles*, on the website of Business in
the Community (www.bitc.org.uk)

Page 61: adapted from *Principles of accounting* by Larry Walther

Page 62: adapted from *The ethical dilemma*, published on the website of the St James
Ethics Centre, Sydney, Australia

Page 63: adapted from *A crucial test for new CPAs: Ethics at the gateway to the profession*
by Jacqueline A. Burke and Jill D'Aquila, reprinted from the CPA journal 2004
with permission from the New York State Society of Certified Public Accountants

Page 66: adapted from *An ethics quiz* by John Raspante, published in eJournal of
Accountancy Online

Page 69: adapted from website of Central Bank of Tunisia

Page 71: adapted and licensed under the GNU Free Documentation Licence from
Wikipedia information

Page 73: adapted from *Malaysia charges three in Transmile accounting fraud case* by
Associated Press, 12th July 2005

Page 78: extract from *UK corporate fraud likely to record high in 2008*, published in
Accountancy Age

Page 92: adapted from manual *ORIGINAL GIM2080 – Accounting framework: general
principles of insurance accounting*, Crown Copyright

Pages 92–93: adapted from Phase II of IFRS for insurance contracts – IASB
discussion paper, reproduced with permission from Deloitte

Page 99 (top): adapted from original statement by the Accounting Standards Board

Page 99 (bottom): adapted from *Insurance sector pays third-highest corporate tax* by
Penny Sukhraj, published in *Accountancy Age*, 8th October 2007

Page 101: adapted from *Extraordinary circumstances: the journey of a corporate
whistleblower* by Cynthia Cooper, published by Sequence Inc.

Every effort has been made to contact copyright holders of material reproduced in
this book. Any omissions will be rectified in subsequent printings if notice is given
to the publisher.

Contents

Introduction

Globalization requires the increased harmonization of financial reporting. Many professions, like accountancy and auditing, have become universal, providing opportunities for those who wish to pursue careers in the international arena.

Such opportunities mean that finance professionals need to be able to communicate effectively with their clients and collegues around the world. As English is widely seen to be the language of international business, employers increasingly require evidence that their employees have reached a high degree of competency in financial English.

The Cambridge ESOL International Certificate in Financial English (ICFE) serves as a benchmark which ensures that people working in the financial sector can communicate effectively in English. Not only are finance professionals required to have a high level of English; it is also vital that they are familiar with the specialist vocabulary and possess the relevant skills to communicate face to face with clients and colleagues, to deliver presentations and to participate in international meetings and conferences.

Absolute Financial English provides practical and stimulating practice material for anyone who requires a solid foundation in financial English and will be welcomed by all candidates preparing for the Cambridge ICFE.

Brigita Schmögnerová
Vice President
Environment, Procurement & Administration
European Bank for Reconstruction and Development

About the ICFE exam

This unit covers:
- Description of the ICFE
- Introduction to the four ICFE papers
- Exam hints
- Time management

DESCRIPTION OF THE ICFE

The Cambridge ESOL International Certificate in Financial English (ICFE) is an examination set at Levels B2 and C1 of the Common European Framework of Reference for Languages and assesses language skills in the context of finance and accounting. B2 is equivalent in level to the Cambridge First Certificate in English, and C1 is equivalent to the Certificate in Advanced English. Examinations at the C1 level may be used as proof of the required level of language to work in the world of international finance and accounting or to follow a course of study related to finance and accountancy at university level.

THE TEST OF READING

In the Test of Reading, you are expected to be able to demonstrate a variety of reading skills, including skimming, scanning, selection of relevant information to complete tasks and deduction of meaning from context. Other essential skills required are speed reading and time management.

Preparing for the Test of Reading

To prepare for the Test of Reading, you need to read a wide range of texts from financial publications, textbooks, web pages and company reports.
You may also find it useful to work with a monolingual dictionary, as this will help you to extend your knowledge of financial collocations and phrases.

> There are six parts in the Test of Reading:
>
> **Part 1** Multiple-choice cloze, with an emphasis on lexis
>
> **Part 2** Open cloze, with an emphasis on structure
>
> **Part 3** Word formation, with an emphasis on lexis
>
> **Part 4** A text preceded by multiple-matching questions
>
> **Part 5** A text from which sentences have been removed and placed in jumbled order after the text
>
> **Part 6** A text followed by four-option multiple-choice questions
>
> 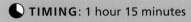 **TIMING**: 1 hour 15 minutes

THE TEST OF READING PARTS 1–3

Parts 1–3 of the exam involve reading a text and completing multiple- or open-cloze tasks using words which fit both grammatically and have the right meaning within the context of the text. The tasks focus on knowledge of vocabulary, such as fixed phrases or collocations, link words and phrasal verbs. In addition, Parts 2 and 3 of the exam focus on grammatical awareness and accuracy of structural items, such as prepositions, pronouns, conjunctions, auxiliaries, etc., and word formation using compounds and affixes.

Part 1: Multiple-choice cloze

This part tests your knowledge of aspects of vocabulary, such as fixed phrases and collocations, shades of meaning, phrasal verbs and link words and phrases.

TIP
Consider all the options before deciding on the answer.

Task	You are required to choose a word or phrase from a set of four (A, B, C or D) to fill a gap in a text. This involves choosing the answer which has the right meaning and fits both grammatically and within the text as a whole.
Consists of ...	two short texts, each containing six items, with an example in the first text.
Total marks	6 (1 mark for each correct answer)

! Several of the options may seem possible, but only one will be correct in that particular context.

Part 2: Open cloze

This part focuses on structure and tests your understanding and control of structural items such as conjunctions, prepositions, pronouns, auxiliaries, quantifiers, etc.

TIP
Look carefully at the words before and after the gap and decide what kind of word is missing (e.g. article, auxiliary verb, preposition, pronoun, conjunction).

Task	You are required to fill the gaps in a text with one word only (in some cases, there may be more than one word which is acceptable, but you should choose only one). This involves choosing the answer which has the right meaning and fits both grammatically as well as within the text.
Consists of ...	a text with 12 gaps, plus one example.
Total marks	12 (1 mark for each correct answer)

!
- Use only one word for each gap.
- Write your answers in CAPITAL LETTERS.
- Remember to check your spelling, as you will be penalised for mistakes.

Part 3: Word formation

This part focuses on vocabulary and tests your ability to form words through affixation and compounding.

TIP
As in Part 2 of the exam, look carefully at the words before and after the gap and decide what kind of word would be appropriate. Then look at the words in the box and consider what words you can form from each one.

Task	You are required to fill the gaps with an appropriate word, formed from a given base word.
Consists of ...	two short texts with six items each.
Total marks	12 (1 mark for each correct answer)

!
- Write your answers in CAPITAL LETTERS.
- Check your spelling.

THE TEST OF READING PARTS 4–6

Parts 4–6 of the exam involve reading a wide range of detailed, finance-related texts, finding relevant details by scanning, understanding complex opinions and arguments, and identifying detail such as implied opinions and attitudes. You will also be required to demonstrate comprehension of a text as a whole and how text structure operates.

Part 4: Multiple matching

TIP
Highlight key words in the questions to help you locate the information in the text.

This part tests your general understanding of a text and your ability to find specific information.

Task	You are required to read questions and scan a text which is divided into four sections, or four short texts. Then you have to match questions with the relevant information from the text. (Some options will need to be used more than once.)
Consists of …	one short text, divided into four sections, or four short texts. There are six questions, with one example.
Total marks	12 (2 marks for each correct answer)

! Do not merely match similar words in the questions with those in the text; match according to meaning.

Part 5: Gapped text

TIP
First of all, read the whole text to get an overall idea of the structure and the meaning of the text. Note the information and ideas that appear before and after each gap.

This part tests your understanding of the structure of texts and your ability to comprehend detailed meaning and argument.

Task	You are required to read a text and to select the sentences which fit the gaps. In each case, only one answer is correct.
Consists of …	a single-page gapped text followed by the options, including one extra sentence which does not fit in any of the gaps. There are six questions.
Total marks	12 (2 marks for each correct answer)

! Check that the sentence you select matches both the sentence before and after the gap.

Part 6: Multiple choice

This part tests your detailed understanding of a text and the opinions and ideas expressed in it.

Task	You are required to read a text and select the most appropriate answers to multiple-choice questions.
Consists of ...	a single-page text followed by multiple-choice questions.
Total	12 (2 marks for each correct answer)

> **!** As in Part 5, do not choose answers based on the meaning of individual words. Look carefully at the development of ideas, outcomes and opinions.

Time management in the Test of Reading

The Test of Reading contains about 2,500 words of text, plus the questions. If you allocate approximate times to each part of the test, this will help you manage your time. Improving your reading speed will also help you to deal with the tasks more quickly and leave you with enough time to check your answers and transfer them to the answer sheet at the end.

Before starting the exam, decide what order you prefer to do the tasks in; you may prefer to start with the longer tasks (Parts 4–6.)

Suggested timing for each part of the Test of Reading	
Part 1	8 minutes
Part 2	8 minutes
Part 3	8 minutes
Part 4	15 minutes
Part 5	15 minutes
Part 6	15 minutes
Transferring your answers	6 minutes

THE TEST OF LISTENING

In this book, the CD track number for each exercise is shown at the start of the exercise.

In the Test of Listening, you are expected to be able to comprehend a variety of listening texts related to finance and accounting. You should be able to listen for gist and detail, and to deduce the opinions and attitude of the speaker. In addition, you must be able to identify and interpret the context of discussions, meetings, presentations, interviews, etc.

Preparing for the Test of Listening

To prepare for the Test of Listening, you need to listen to discussions, interviews and presentations. The Web is a good source of authentic material, and you will find many podcasts of presentations and interviews on the websites of accounting bodies, universities, accounting firms and banks and financial institutions.

There are four parts in the Test of Listening:

Part 1 Three short, unrelated extracts from monologues or exchanges between interacting speakers, each followed by two three-option multiple-choice questions.

Part 2 A text involving interacting speakers, followed by three-option multiple-choice questions.

Part 3 A sentence-completion task based on a monologue.

Part 4 Five short, related extracts from monologues followed by two multiple-matching tasks.

⏱ **TIMING**: 40 minutes

Part 1: Multiple choice

TIP
As you listen, focus on the questions (rather than the options) and listen for the answer in the recording. Then try to match this with the nearest option.

This part tests your ability to listen a text in detail, including your understanding of the opinions and ideas expressed in it. It consists of three short, unrelated extracts from monologues or exchanges between interacting speakers, each followed by two three-option multiple-choice questions.

Part 2: Multiple choice

This part of the test consists of a text involving interacting speakers, followed by three-option multiple-choice questions. The questions on the page follow the order of that in the recording.

Part 3: Sentence completion

TIP
Use the pause between the first and second listening to check your answers.
Check that each answer makes sense by looking at the wording both before and after the gap.

This part of the test consists of a sentence-completion task based on a monologue. The questions on the page follow the order of that in the recording.

 Check your spelling.

Part 4: Multiple matching

TIP
Read through both tasks before your hear the recording for the first time.

This part of the test consists of five short, related extracts from monologues followed by two multiple-matching tasks.

 Remember that there are two tasks in this section and that you may hear the answer to Task 2 before that of Task 1.

THE TEST OF SPEAKING

In the Test of Speaking, you are expected to be able to perform a variety of spoken tasks on topics related to finance and accounting. At the same time, you must be able to demonstrate interactional, social, transactional, negotiation and collaborative skills.

Preparing for the Test of Speaking

To prepare for the Test of Speaking, you need to practise talking about accounting and financial issues as much as possible. In order to get the most out of discussions in class, you need to participate actively and use every opportunity to encourage other members of the group to become involved.

There are four parts in the Test of Speaking:

Part 1 You will be asked to talk about yourself by responding to the examiner's questions.

Part 2 You will be given a choice of two topics accompanied by written prompts. You select one of the topics and give a short presentation for about one minute. The other candidate responds as instructed.

Part 3 You and the other candidate talk together, working towards a negotiated completion of a task.

Part 4 The examiner leads a discussion with you and the other candidate.

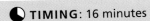 **TIMING:** 16 minutes

Part 1: Interview

TIP
Try to give natural answers to the questions; do not respond with 'speeches'.

In this part of the test, you are asked to talk about yourself by responding to the examiner's questions. This is your first chance to introduce yourself to the examiner, so it is important to relax and focus on giving clear and confident answers. Try to manage your nerves and concentrate on providing full answers to the examiner's questions.

Part 2: Long turn

TIP
Listen carefully to your partner's long turn and respond as instructed by the examiner.

In this part of the test, you are given a choice of two topics to talk about, accompanied by written prompts. You select one of the topics and give a short presentation for about one minute. Then the other candidate asks a question about your talk, which you answer.

In this part of the exam, it is important that you are confident about speaking on a variety of finance-related topics. You don't have to be an expert on every topic, but you need to be able to provide a brief introduction to the topic and express your opinions about it clearly.

Part 3: Collaborative task

TIP
Discuss each aspect of the task in detail before concluding.

In this part of the Test of Speaking, you and another person take part in a discussion together and work towards the negotiated completion of a task.

Part 4: Discussion

TIP
In all parts of the test, develop the discussion as much as possible and use a wide a range of language and vocabulary.

In this part of the test, the examiner leads a discussion with you and another candidate, based on questions related to the task in Part 3.

THE TEST OF WRITING

In the Test of Writing, you are expected to be able to complete writing tasks covering a range of finance- and accounting-related topics in response to the prompts provided and for a specific target reader and purpose.

The two parts of the exam require you to write a letter and a report.

> There are two parts in the Test of Writing:
>
> **Part 1** One question requiring the production of a letter.
>
> **Part 2** One question requiring the production of a short report.
>
> **TIMING**: 1 hour 15 minutes

Preparing for the Test of Writing

To prepare for the Test of Writing, you need plenty of practice in thinking about planning, drafting and editing writing tasks.

ACTION PLAN

1 Brainstorm common topics in accounting. Make lists of key issues or questions and draft short reports including the main points.

2 Summarise articles from financial newspapers or magazines.

3 Write short descriptions of financial concepts and related questions and examples.

4 Create topics for correspondence and write letters for both parties.

5 Read and paraphrase short texts.

6 Adopt the habit of writing every day.

7 Edit your own writing.

8 Follow up your presentation by writing a brief summary of the main points.

9 Identify your common errors and focus on getting rid of them.

10 Improve your accuracy; reread and edit constantly.

11 Edit each other's writing in class and outside and provide feedback.

12 Discuss your writing with your trainer.

13 Work on improving your time management of writing tasks.

14 Keep a daily journal to which you add something every day.

15 Collect examples of good writing and follow their style.

Time management in the Test of Writing

As in any exam, in the ICFE you have a limited amount of time to read, plan, complete and check your answers. Hence you need to manage your time so that you have sufficient time for both sections, Task 1 and 2.

TASK 1
Spend 20 minutes on this task:
- 5 minutes preparing
- 10 minutes writing the letter
- 5 minutes checking and editing

TASK 2
Spend 55 minutes on this task:
- 10–15 minutes preparing
- 30 minutes writing the report
- 10–15 minutes checking and editing

Part 1: Letter

This part of the test requires the production of a letter.

Part 2: Report

This part of the test requires the production of a short report.

TIPS
Part 1
- Read the opening paragraphs and instructions and highlight key words.
- Think carefully about your role and the purpose of the task, whom you are writing to and what you are trying to achieve in the task.
- You may use key words in your answer, but do not lift whole sections from from the task instructions.

TIPS
Part 2
- Make sure you cover all four points of the task.
- Consider the 'balance' of your answer. Some parts of the question may require a brief answer, others may need more detail.

Introduction to ICFE

This unit covers:

TOPICS
- Accuracy of accounts
- The balance sheet
- Accounting standards
- The image of accountants
- History of accounting

SKILLS
- Reading: Deducing missing words, word formation, retrieving specific information
- Listening: Listening for gist, listening for detail,
- Speaking: Responding to questions, collaborative discussions, mini-presentations,
- Writing: Improving writing skills, dealing with errors, letter/report writing

READING

■ Section A Skills

TALKING POINT

Discuss these questions.

1 How has the role of accountants changed in recent years?

2 What's the difference between a Financial Analyst and an Accountant?

1 Rate your reading skills

Before you tackle the Test of Reading, consider your current reading skills. Look at the list below and tick the skills mentioned according to your degree of competence.

A Very well   **B** Quite well   **C** Satisfactorily   **D** Not well enough

How well can you ...	A	B	C	D
1 identify the purpose of reading?				
2 form a general impression by skimming a text?				
3 predict the content of an article?				
4 retrieve specific information by scanning a text?				
5 understand technical vocabulary?				
6 manage your time while you are reading?				
7 demonstrate your understanding of text as a whole?				
8 interpret a text for inference and attitude?				
9 deduce meaning from the context?				
10 select the relevant language to complete a text?				
11 form collocations?				
12 follow linking words and signposts in a text?				
13 select relevant information to perform a task?				
14 demonstrate understanding of how text structure operates?				
15 interpret the contents of an article from its title?				
16 read quickly and effectively?				
17 interpret instructions?				
18 highlight key points in a text?				
19 pace your reading – mixing skimming and scanning?				
20 maintain your concentration while reading?				

Discuss your choices with a partner.

2 Deduction skills

In this text, some of the words have been replaced with names of cities. Look carefully at the sentences to deduce what word was used in the original. Discuss your answers with a partner.

CONCERN ABOUT ACCURACY OF FINANCIAL ACCOUNTS

In the USA, following the Enron **(1) Budapest**, there has been substantial **(2) São Paulo** about the accuracy of financial statements. CEOs and CFOs are personally liable for attesting that financial statements 'do not contain any **(3) Dublin** statement of a material fact or omit to state a material fact **(4) Berlin** to make the statements made, in light of the circumstances under which such statements were made, not misleading with respect to the period **(5) Santiago** by the report'. If misleading or inaccurate financial statements are compiled, it exposes the people involved to substantial civil and criminal liability. One example of such a case is when Bernie Ebbers, former CEO of WorldCom, was **(6) Buenos Aires** to 25 years in federal prison for allowing the company's revenue to be overstated by $11 billion over a five-year period.

3 Missing words

TIP
Look carefully at the words before and after each gap and make sure your answers have the right meaning and fit grammatically in the text.

Read the following extract from a case study about using the balance sheet. Think of the best word to fill each gap. The first one **(0)** is given as an example.

How a good balance sheet helped me to improve my business

Sandeep Sud is a qualified solicitor **(0)** _who_ also runs a school uniform business based in Hounslow, **(1)** _____ partnership with his parents. The company, which has four full-time employees, uses **(2)** _____ balance sheet to gauge how the business is progressing. It **(3)** _____ also been a key factor in securing a bank loan for the improvement and expansion of the company premises.

'**(4)** _____ a partnership, we produce a balance sheet as part of our annual accounts and as an internal management exercise. **(5)** _____ , a balance sheet gives a snapshot of how the business is doing at a particular time. **(6)** _____ this is useful, you have to remember that it **(7)** _____ change overnight. For example, if you were in debt on April 30 when you did **(8)** _____ year-end accounts, but paid this off on May 1, you would get a **(9)** _____ different picture of the strength of the business.

(10) _____ , the balance sheet is useful when looked at alongside the profit-and-loss figures because then you get the whole picture. If you borrowed a lot in one particular year, **(11)** _____ had made a profit, the profit would show on your profit-and-loss accounts. **(12)** _____ , the amount you owed would only be apparent on the balance sheet. It's important to be aware of both sets of numbers.'

■ Section B Exam focus

1 Word formation

Look at the words in the box on the right. With a partner, discuss how many words you can form from each one. Then decide which words fit in the same numbered gaps in the text. Write the words in CAPITAL LETTERS.

On its (**1**) _____ , the IASB made a
(**2**) _____ that the IASC Foundation Trustees
agreed that accounting standards issued by IASB would be
designated 'International Financial Reporting Standards'
and (**3**) _____ their decision in a press release
dated 23 April 2001. On 23 May 2002, the IASB made an
(**4**) _____ regarding the publication of the
Preface to International Financial Reporting Standards.
Sir David Tweedie, IASB Chairman, said this document
provided 'a brief (**5**) _____ of the purpose
and function of the main structures of the new
(**6**) _____ for setting global standards'.
Following this, the first IFRS was published in June 2003
(IFRS 1).

| 1 FORM |
| 2 STATE |
| 3 PROMULGATE |
| 4 ANNOUNCE |
| 5 DESCRIBE |
| 6 ARRANGE |

2 Multiple-choice cloze

Read this extract from a statement about the sub-prime crisis. Choose the best word or phrase (A, B, C or D) to fill each gap. The first one (**0**) is given as an example.

'When written in Chinese, the word "crisis" is composed of two characters. One represents danger and the other represents opportunity.'
John F. Kennedy

危
機

FINANCIAL REPORTING ISSUES ARISING FROM THE SUB-PRIME CRISIS

Over the last few years, many capital and other financial (**0**) _markets_ have experienced considerable (**1**) _____ . These difficulties, which would appear to be the result of problems that started in the US subprime (**2**) _____ sector in 2007, have had a number of consequences, both for companies and for markets. Steps are now being taken to (**3**) _____ confidence.

At such times, it is essential that (**4**) _____ action is taken to ensure that the interests of European (**5**) _____ are looked after properly. While we do not believe that financial reporting has caused the crisis as some have (**6**) _____ , we do believe it is essential that a comprehensive (**7**) _____ is carried out of existing external financial reporting requirements to determine whether any of those requirements has intensified some or all of the problems that have arisen.

	A		B		C		D	
0	A instruments		B tools		C markets		D institutions
1	A turmoil		B bankruptcies		C decline		D difficulties
2	A mortgage		B lending		C losses		D capital
3	A establish		B reestablish		C rise		D recover
4	A timely		B strict		C swift		D appropriate
5	A members		B investors		C stakeholders		D players
6	A claimed		B underlined		C blamed		D commented
7	A report		B study		C statement		D review

3 Topic sentences

In the article below about the stereotype image of accountants, the first sentence of each paragraph is missing. Read the article, paying close attention to the words that follow each gap, then match these sentences (A–F) with the correct paragraph (1–5). There is one extra sentence which you do not need to use.

A The stereotypical views about accountants seem to be firmly set in people's minds.

B At Kingston Smith, we have a number of initiatives to encourage greater understanding about the reality of the profession, from partners giving talks at local schools to a summer-holiday scheme allowing university students to gain an insight into the reality of the profession before committing to a career in this area.

C Instead of accepting such damning criticism, we should be doing everything we can to promote the message that accountants are at the heart of business and can play a key role in the strategic development of a business.

D In a recent study, scientists at City University of Hong Kong have proved that the belief that accountants are boring is actually true.

E Why is accountancy still considered to be so dull?

F However, further analysis revealed that accountancy still has a major image problem, especially when compared to other professional career choices.

It's time for the profession to tackle stereotypes of accountants

1 _____

Kingston Smith recently commissioned research into career choices and perceptions about our profession. It was encouraging to see that, of 48 different career options, accountancy ranked as the fourth most popular career choice – more popular than teaching, HR, engineering, marketing, journalism, veterinary surgery, catering and hairdressing – and was equally popular amongst men and women.

2 _____

Twice as many people wanted to go into law or medicine as accountancy. We clearly have a long way to go to persuade people that accountancy can be an exciting and challenging career option.

3 _____

Until they are addressed, we will continue to be considered an inferior profession when compared to medicine or law, deterring many strong candidates. Our research indicates that the overriding personality trait associated with accountants is that we are boring. Almost half of those polled thought this was the case, with 28% believing us to lack a sense of humour, and only 4% perceiving accountants to be fun.

4 _____

We all know that accountants need far wider skills than just an aptitude for numbers, but we must continually communicate this externally. Anyone in practice knows that we wouldn't attract any new clients if we couldn't relate to people.

5 _____

Maybe we need to go a stage further, however. We all need to be more accountable for our image problem. Is it time for a sustained PR campaign, perhaps organised by the ICAEW with direct input from the top 20 firms? What else can we all be doing together to tackle this ongoing issue?

'Some people think accountants are just boring number crunchers … but actually 47% of 235 people covering 34% of the demographic profile thought that 39% of accountants were …'

www.CartoonStock.com

LISTENING

■ Section A **Skills**

1 Pre-listening

What do you know about the history of accounting? Look at the quiz and, with a partner, decide if the statements are true or false.

HISTORY OF ACCOUNTING QUIZ

1 The first textbook on accounting was written in the 13th century.

2 The calculator was invented in the late 19th century.

3 Bankers in Babylon recorded transactions on stone tablets in 1000 BCE.

4 Evidence suggests that double-bookkeeping was used by the Romans.

5 In 1772, Joseph Wedgewood saved his firm from the recession by applying cost-accounting methods.

6 Accountants were first registered as 'accomptants' in England at the end of the 18th century.

7 The modern cost-accounting system was invented by William Cooper in 1854.

8 Amatino Manucci is said to have been the first 'real' accountant.

'Forensic scientists have now determined that the fall of the Roman Empire was due to an accounting error.'

---

2 🎧 2 1.1 Listening for gist

Listen to a student opening his presentation about the history of accounting. Tick the topic this part of his speech is about.

A The start of accounting standards ☐

B The man who invented accounting ☐

C The importance of accounting ☐

3 🎧 2 1.1 Listening for detail

Listen again, and complete these sentences.

1 Venice used to be _____ in the Renaissance period.

2 Pacioli was often referred to as _____ .

3 Pacioli studied as _____ .

4 One of his friends at the time was _____ .

5 His book provided a summary of _____ .

6 The Summa presented the idea of _____ .

7 One of Pacioli's suggestions was that a trial balance should _____ .

8 Other subjects Pacioli referred to were ethics, _____ .

■ Section B **Exam focus**

1 Pre-listening

Look at the book cover below. With a partner, discuss what you expect to hear about this book.

EXAM TASK
Test of Listening Part 4

2 🎧 📖 3–7 1.2–1.6 **Multiple matching**

TASK ONE: REASON FOR BUYING THE BOOK

Listen to five people talking about a book on accounting standards. As you listen, choose from the list (A–F) the reason each speaker gives for buying the book. One reason is not mentioned by any of the speakers.

SPEAKER

A Had difficulty understanding accounting standards _____

B As background reading for a short introductory talk _____

C In preparation of a seminar and discussion group _____

D Needed a book with a strong, graphic style _____

E To write a report about accounting standards _____

F Someone at work suggested getting the book. _____

TASK TWO: BENEFITS OF READING THE BOOK

Listen again and choose from the list (A–F) the main benefit of the reading the book for each speaker. One benefit is not mentioned by any of the speakers.

SPEAKER

A Written in a clear, simple style – not technical _____

B Each chapter provides an overview of key issues. _____

C Provides solutions to problems with accounting standards _____

D Provides up-to-date information _____

E Is easy to find information in the book _____

F Contains excellent graphics which aid memory _____

3 Read and check

Now read the audio transcripts (page 121) and highlight the parts in which the speakers refer to the benefits of reading the book. Then discuss them with your partner.

SPEAKING

■ Section A Skills

1 Improving your speaking skills

In order to improve your discussion and presentation skills, use every opportunity both inside and outside the classroom to practise your speaking.

1 Practise speaking every day about a finance-related topic.

2 Expand your use of language for expressing your ideas and opinions.

3 Record yourself speaking every day.

4 Practise the pronunciation of difficult technical words.

5 Listen to podcasts about finance, then try to recreate them.

6 Create a weekly topics log and practise giving simple presentations.

7 Read snippets of financial news and talk about them.

8 Practise explaining several financial terms every day.

Now, with a partner, discuss other ways of improving your speaking skills.

Being an effective group member

- Listen to other students and offer your comments.
  Well, I hadn't thought of that …
- Include everyone in the group.
  What do you think about that?
- Show your agreement.
  Exactly …
- Encourage the group to keep to the point.
  I'm not sure that's relevant.
- Add your comments to other people's views.
  That's interesting.
- Encourage other speakers.
  That's a good point.
- Offer suggestions.
  Shall we …?
- Stop interruptions.
  May I go on?
- Sum up.
  Well, we are agreed on that, then.

---

2 Discussion

Talk to your partner about each of the topics below for two minutes. After two minutes, your partner will continue the discussion.

1 Many people believe that accounting is dull.

2 Accounting has changed significantly in the past few years.

3 Some of the negative impacts of corporate accounting scandals are …

4 There is a shortage of accountants these days.

5 Bankruptcy accounting is interesting because …

6 If I were aware that a client had manipulated his/her accounting figures, …

7 The most difficult tasks facing an accountant are …

8 Employers should have a process in place that allows employees to report questionable accounting if …

■ Section B Exam focus

EXAM TASK
Test of Speaking Part 1

'Questions are never indiscreet. Answers sometimes are.'
Oscar Wilde

1 Responding to questions

With a partner, ask and answer these questions in turn. Then discuss what you think would be the best answer for each question.

- What interests you most about your present job?
- What would you like to be doing in five years' time?
- What are your biggest successes professionally?
- What would you like to change in the firm you work for?
- What is the worst part of your job?
- What qualities does a good accountant have?
- Tell me something about your education.
- Tell me something about the firm you work for.
- Tell me something about your work experience.
- Tell me something about your boss.

Good/bad answers

I don't know.
I've never really thought about it. } = BAD
I'm not sure really.

Well, I'm not an expert in this field, but I think … } = GOOD
In my opinion … / In my view, … / Personally, I think …

- Relax and focus on giving clear, confident answers.
- Give full answers to the examiner's questions.

2 Collaborative discussion

With a partner, discuss what qualities make a good accountant and list five essential qualities. Then report back to the group.

  See **Language bank, Discussions**, page 118

3 One-minute presentations

Look at these questions and discuss your opinions with a partner. Both of you will give a one-minute presentation of your views on each question in turn.

1 In today's corporate environment, do you feel that accountants are the 'conscience of last resort'?

2 How often do you feel pressure from clients to manipulate the figures in your work?

3 Should the term 'accountant' be regulated so as to limit those who can use the term?

4 Is the government in your country doing enough to address the skills-shortage crisis in accountancy?

TIPS
1 Speak clearly.
2 Use the KISS principle (Keep It Short and Simple).
3 Provide a clear introduction, middle and end.
4 Use clear signposting language to guide listeners through your presentation.

See **Language bank, Presentations**, page 118

WRITING

■ Section A **Skills**

1 Improving your writing

Look at the topics below and, with a partner, make of list of three reasons for each one. Then spend five minutes writing about each topic, introducing each one and outlining the reasons.

REASONS …

- that I decided to study accounting.
- for the standardisation of accounting standards.
- for both internal and external auditing.
- that companies experience cashflow problems.
- that accounting is becoming more attractive as a profession.

2 Keeping an error log

Whether you are writing a short or long piece of writing, get into the habit of editing your own work and keep a log of the types of mistakes you make.

Swap the introductions you wrote above with a partner and edit them using these symbols. Discuss what are your most common errors.

Type of error	Symbol
tense	T
word order	WO
wrong word/phrase	WW
spelling	SP
other	O

3 Error workshop

Choose a couple of your own 'favourite' errors and write them on pieces of paper. Swap your errors with other members of the group and, as you do so, correct the errors on the slips of paper.

'So now people from all around the world know you can't spell.'

TRIVIA

J.P. Morgan, the American financier and banker, started with a degree in accounting.

■ Section B **Exam focus**

1 Creating your own writing task for Part 1

With a partner, create a letter-writing task. Use this template to help you.

- TYPE OF LETTER
- FROM _____
- TO _____
- DESCRIPTION OF TASK

Write a letter to ...
Include the following points in your letter:
- _____
- _____
- _____
- _____

EXAM TASK
Test of Writing Part-2

TIP
Before you start writing:
- read the exam question carefully
- underline the most important parts
- ask yourself:
  – What is the purpose of the task?
  – Who am I writing to?
  – What exactly is my role?
- make sure you cover all the points required.

2 Report

Your client is considering outsourcing some of its internal accounting and bookkeeping and would like some general advice in relation to this. In a brief report, give the client some initial advice on two of the following points and explain what information you would need to take on these tasks.

- Handling cashflow
- Management accounting
- Preparing forecasts/budgets
- Dealing with payroll

Write 200–250 words in an appropriate style.

▶ See **Language bank**, **Linking ideas** and **Handling questions**, page 119

3 Creating your own writing task for Part 2

With a partner, create a similar writing task.

Time management

1 Preparation (10–15 mins)

2 Writing the report (30 mins)

3 Checking and editing (10–15 mins)

The financial environment

READING

■ Section A   Skills

TALKING POINT

Discuss these questions.

1 What is the IASB?

2 What is its primary function?

3 What are IFRSs?

1 Vocabulary guessing

Before reading, guess the meaning of the words on the left (1–9) and match them with similar expressions on the right (a–i).

1 concepts	**a** incorporated
2 adopted	**b** announcements
3 pronouncements	**c** dealing with
4 highlights	**d** objectives
5 external	**e** structure
6 compiled	**f** publishes
7 issues	**g** prepared
8 resolving	**h** outside
9 framework	**i** underlines

2 Deducing vocabulary from context

Complete this text by replacing the items of office equipment in bold with the words 1–9 in Exercise 1.

> The IASB's (**1**) **photocopier** for the Preparation and Presentation of Financial Statements describes the basic (**2**) **chairs** by which financial statements are (**3**) **keyboard** and presented for (**4**) **flipchart** users. The Framework serves as a guide to (**5**) **desk** accounting issues that are not addressed directly in a standard. It also (**6**) **calculator** the qualitative characteristics that make information in financial statements useful.
>
> The IASB (**7**) **telephone** its standards in a series of (**8**) **computers** called International Financial Reporting Standards. It has also (**9**) **printer** the body of standards issued by the Board of the International Accounting Standards Commitee (IASC).

■ Section B **Exam focus**

EXAM TASK
Test of Reading Part 1A

1 Gap fill

Read the description of chartered accountancy below. Choose the best word or phrase to fill each gap from the box. The first one (**0**) is given as an example.

> **TIP**
> Part 1 of the Test of Reading, your task is to complete two modified-cloze texts, each containing six gaps, followed by six four-option multiple-choice items.

| aim | assume | expertise | insolvency | ~~involves~~ | range | solid |

WHAT IS CHARTERED ACCOUNTANCY?

Chartered accountancy (**0**) _involves_ giving professional advice to organisations on a wide (**1**) _____ of business and finance issues. Chartered accountants (**2**) _____ the role of business advisers, making high-level strategic decisions that (**3**) _____ to improve profitability and increase market share for their clients' or their employer's businesses. Many chartered accountants also go on to use their (**4**) _____ to set up businesses of their own, becoming successful entrepreneurs. As well as financial reporting, taxation, auditing, forensic accounting, corporate finance and (**5**) _____ , accountants are expected to have a (**6**) _____ foundation in business, marketing, economics, finance, management and information systems.

EXAM TASK
Test of Reading Part 1B

2 Multiple choice

Read this extract from an article about the changing world of accounting. Choose the best word or phrase (A, B, C or D) to fill each gap. The first one (**0**) is given as an example.

> **TIP**
> What texts are used in Part 1?
> Chiefly extracts from reference books and financial textbooks, financial newspapers and journals, financial websites, company annual reports, and correspondence.

THE CHANGING FACE OF ACCOUNTING

'Welcome to the new world of accounting.' These words have for some time featured in the (**0**) _foreword_ to numerous articles on the subject of the International Accounting Standards Board's (IASB's) International Financial Reporting Standards (IFRS). They also may well be the (**1**) _____ shared by finance and other staff of an estimated 7,000 (**2**) _____ companies in the European Union (EU) who soon will be required to (**3**) _____ with the standards.

(**4**) _____ , the last two years may prove to have been pivotal in the saga of global accounting (**5**) _____ . In a world recovering from corporate scandal, fraudulent financial reporting and economic decline in recent years, the value of common ground is (**6**) _____ . Having a single, global set of high-quality accounting standards would benefit investors and reduce the administrative costs of accessing capital markets around the world.

0	A follow-up	B announcement	C (foreword)	D conclusion
1	A sentiment	B assumption	C responsibility	D judgement
2	A private	B listed	C audited	D assessed
3	A follow	B adopt	C meet	D comply
4	A Perhaps	B However	C Additionally	D Indeed
5	A frauds	B standards	C laws	D developments
6	A unclear	B required	C transparent	D clearly

LISTENING

■ Section A **Skills**

1 🎧 ⑧ **2.1 Listening to figures**

Listen to the start of a presentation about the Institute of Chartered Accountants of Scotland (ICAS). Circle the figures you hear (between one and four figures in each set).

a 1834   1854   1934   1954

b 34%   56%   66%   83%   94%

c 2,400   2,404   3,014   3,440   16,000

d 94%   95%   49%   98%

2 🎧 ⑧ **2.1 Note-taking**

Listen again and make notes about each figure the speaker mentions.

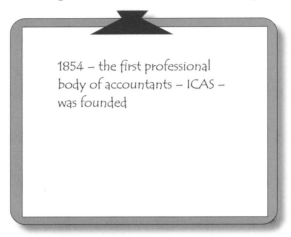

1854 – the first professional body of accountants – ICAS – was founded

3 🎧 ⑧ **2.1 Sentence completion**

Complete these sentences with a partner. Then listen again and check your answers.

1 The purpose of the presentation is to …

2 ICAS was the first …

3 The high growth rate makes ICAS …

4 🎧 ⑨ **2.2 Note-taking**

Listen to a student talking to a training provider at an educational fair and complete these notes.

Requirements for training as a CA: _____

_____

No. of training vacancies (UK): _____

_____

Employers are looking for _____

_____

Exemptions from exams: _____

▶ See **Useful abbreviations**, pages 116–117

■ Section B Exam focus

TIP
In the Test of Listening, you will have 15 seconds to look at the questions before you listen to each section.

TIP
In Parts 1 and 2 of the Test of Listening, you will sometimes be asked to answer questions about the speakers' opinions or feelings.

EXAM TASK
Test of Listening Part 2

1 🎧 **10** 2.3 **Listening for gist**

Listen to the extract, in which five graduates are talking to a career adviser about job applications. First of all, establish what the speakers are talking about and circle the correct topic.

A How to write a good CV

B The importance of covering letters

C How to respond to questions on the application form

2 🎧 **10** 2.3 **Listening to deduce opinions**

Listen again and write the name of the graduate (Tony, Chanelle, Aydin, Hans or Sophie) who uses each of these phrases from the conversation.

1 I'm not sure about that.

2 Exactly.

3 I agree.

4 If you ask me, I think …

5 I'm not convinced that's true.

3 🎧 **11** 2.4 **Multiple choice**

Listen to the next part of the conversation between the graduates. For questions 1–6, choose the best answer (A, B or C). Listen to the recording twice.

1 According to Chanelle, the letter should …
  A have a good opening paragraph.
  B consist of no more than three paragraphs.
  C contain all the relevant work experience.

2 According to Aydin, in a covering letter you should …
  A write concisely.
  B introduce yourself to the employer.
  C provide details of your education.

3 Hans mentions that the letter should …
  A demonstrate why you are suited to the job.
  B not be long-winded.
  C clarify the details on your CV.

4 Sophie underlines the importance of …
  A explaining your suitability for the job.
  B making an impact with your letter.
  C writing a detailed letter.

5 Tony mentions that …
  A the letter should sound confident.
  B style is not important.
  C a degree of formality is required.

6 Aydin and Chanelle add comments on the importance of paying attention to …
  A layout and spelling names correctly.
  B checking the address.
  C enclosing the CV.

4 🎧 **12** 2.5 **Listening and speaking**

Listen to a financial adviser talking about the qualitative characteristics of accounting information and answer these questions.

1 What does the statement cover?

2 What is the FASB's role?

3 What factors influence decision-makers' judgement in the last analysis of accounts?

4 What is the most significant question about the decision-maker?

▶ See **Useful abbreviations**, pages 116–117

SPEAKING

■ Section A **Skills**

1 Opening a presentation

Choose one of these topics and prepare to introduce a presentation to the group. In your presentation, follow the checklist below.

1 advantages / disadvantages of EU harmonisation
2 problems choosing accountancy software
3 your daily responsibilities / tasks at work
4 the importance of external and internal audits

CHECKLIST
- Greet the audience
- Thank your audience for coming
- Introduce yourself
- Introduce the main topic
- Outline the main points

TIP
The audience will only remember three messages from your presentation. Plan them in advance.

2 Presenting three points

Continue the presentations you started in Exercise 1 and introduce three points you want to get across to your audience.

The 'rule of three' is based on the concept that people remember things when they are in listed in threes. It is particularly used by advertisers who know the value of using the 'rule of three' to sell their ideas.

Blood, sweat and tears.

There was an Englishman, an Irishman and a Scotsman …

The good, the bad and the ugly.

3 Mini-presentation

Your trainer will give you some information about a financial institution, association or qualification. You have ten minutes to read and prepare a one-minute presentation about it.

▶ See **Language bank, Presentions**, page 118

■ Section B Exam focus

TIP
In Part 1 of the Test of Speaking, you will be asked some questions about yourself.

1 Talking about your present job

In small groups, discuss how you would answer these questions.

- What is your current position?
- What do you like about your job?
- If you could, what would you like to change in your firm?
- How do you get on with the other people at work?
- What elements of your job are you not keen on?
- Where would you like to be in five years' time?
- What other qualifications would you like to gain?
- Is there another field of accounting that you would like to pursue?
- What is the most/least interesting part of your job?
- Do you envisage staying with your present employer?

TIP
In Part 4 of the exam, you will have to talk for three minutes.

2 Three-minute discussion

With a partner, discuss the topics on the discussion sheet. Expand each topic as much as possible and add additional information or questions.

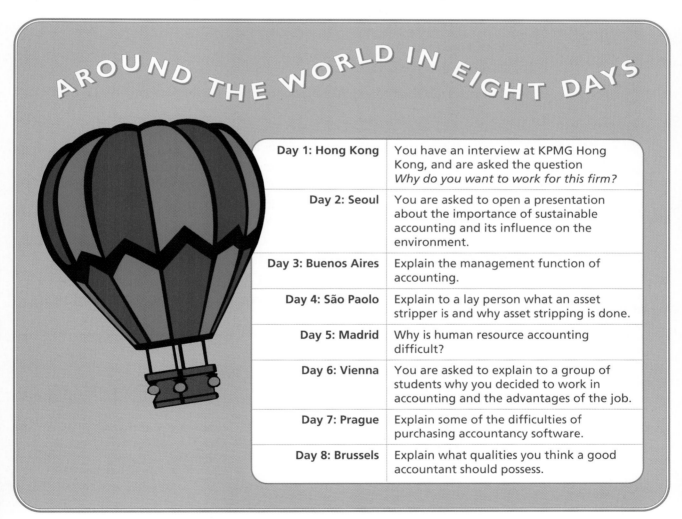

AROUND THE WORLD IN EIGHT DAYS

Day 1: Hong Kong	You have an interview at KPMG Hong Kong, and are asked the question *Why do you want to work for this firm?*
Day 2: Seoul	You are asked to open a presentation about the importance of sustainable accounting and its influence on the environment.
Day 3: Buenos Aires	Explain the management function of accounting.
Day 4: São Paolo	Explain to a lay person what an asset stripper is and why asset stripping is done.
Day 5: Madrid	Why is human resource accounting difficult?
Day 6: Vienna	You are asked to explain to a group of students why you decided to work in accounting and the advantages of the job.
Day 7: Prague	Explain some of the difficulties of purchasing accountancy software.
Day 8: Brussels	Explain what qualities you think a good accountant should possess.

▶ See **Language bank, Discussions,** page 118

WRITING

■ Section A **Skills**

TIP

In the Test of Writing (Task 1), you are asked to write a formal letter.

1 Formal writing

Look at these sentences and decide whether they come from the introduction or the conclusion of a letter. Which expressions do you think are informal?

1 We act as the accountants to Hogg Limited, established in 1974.

2 I am writing to you on behalf of Brian Jones, owner of Acorn Publishing.

3 If you require further information, please do not hesitate to contact me.

4 I refer to my client's financial statements.

5 Please ring me when you have a moment.

6 Further to your recent request, please find enclosed a copy of my accounts.

7 I am writing in response to your query regarding my client's legal status.

8 In short, Clearbright Limited continues to show acceptable levels of profitability.

9 I will pop the documents in the post tomorrow.

10 I hope the points outlined above clarify the situation.

11 I look forward to hearing from you.

12 Finally, let's meet next week to have a chat about the report.

2 Opening phrases

Write the first line of these letters.

1 A letter to a bank confirming that your firm acts as the accountants to Ecofarms Limited.

2 A letter of application to a firm of accountants in response to an advertisement for a job as an accountant advertised in *Financial World*.

3 A letter to the Auditing Committee stating that you have been appointed to audit the consolidated financial statements of Redgrove Care Limited.

4 A letter confirming your receipt of an invitation to attend an interview at the University of Brighton at 10.30 a.m. next Friday.

3 Self-editing skills

TIP

In the exam, it is important that you set aside some time at the end to reread and check the accuracy of your writing.

Look at the letter of application on the next page; it contains several mistakes. With a partner, decide how you would correct and improve it. Use these checklists to help you.

SELF-EDITING CHECKLISTS

Accuracy
- Are the verbs in the correct tenses?
- Are any prepositions missing?
- Any spelling mistakes or inconsistent spelling?
- Is the punctuation in the right place?

Style
- Is the writing divided into a clear and logical sequence of paragraphs?
- Is there a clear introduction and conclusion to the writing?
- Does the writing have a logical sequence?
- Is the style formal and neutral?

---

4 Rewriting

Rewrite the same letter, correcting the mistakes.

Mrs Jane Harris
Cook, Green and Clarkson
152 Roman Road
Hove
BN21 9HL

Dear Mrs Harris,

I apply for the position of Chief Accountant that advertised in the *Financial Times*, 3 January 2008.
I currently a senior accountant position with full responsibility for the monthly profit and loss statement of the Infinity Foods Limited. Actually, in the last five years of my accounting experience has always been with food industry.
Enclosed is my CV. I will be glad to discuss my qualification in an interview.

Best,

[signature]
[name]
[title]

Enclosure: CV

■ Section B Exam focus

EXAM TASK
Test of Writing Part 1

1 Letter of application

Write a similar letter of application to the one in section A. In your letter, include information about your:

● education
● qualifications
● work experience
● current position

TIP
In Part 1 of the Test of Writing, you are asked to write a letter.
Spend 20 minutes on this task: 5 minutes on preparation, 10 minutes writing the letter and 5 minutes checking and editing.

2 Editing

When you have finished, swap letters with a partner and edit each other's letters.

3 Follow-up

With a partner, discuss the common errors in each other's letter and report back to the group. Make notes on the notepad below of errors to avoid for future reference. Share and compare your common errors with other members of the group.

ERRORS LOG
Date
1
2
3

Accounting systems

This unit covers:

TOPICS
- Accounting software
- Accounting qualifications
- Accounting interviews

SKILLS
- Reading: sequencing a text, speed reading, summarizing
- Listening: listening and note-taking, identifying speakers' opinions
- Speaking: handling interview questions, delivering mini-presentations
- Writing: introduction to letter writing

READING

■ Section A Skills

TALKING POINT

Before reading, consider these questions and discuss them with a partner.

1 What do you think is the key feature to look for when evaluating accounting software?

2 What problems do customers often have when they want to upgrade accounting software?

1 Sequencing a text

This text is jumbled up. With a partner, put the sentences in the correct order. Use these signposts to help you: *Thirdly, Next, also, At this stage, Finally …*

> **Choosing the right software**
>
> **A** Finally, in addition to requesting external assistance, your accountant, who is familiar with your situation, will be able to assist you throughout the process of selecting a suitable product.
>
> **B** It is also a good idea to consider upgrading your hardware if it would not be able to cope.
>
> **C** Next, decide on a realistic budget and calculate what funds are available.
>
> **D** Thirdly, consult your Information Technology staff (or computer consultant) and obtain their advice regarding technologies that match your current equipment and abilities.
>
> **E** Obviously, hiring an impartial third party or consultant also helps you to evaluate your needs and select a suitable product.
>
> **F** Before choosing software, you should look at your current accounting system and identify existing problems and needs that are not adequately met.
>
> **G** It is advisable to obtain feedback from everyone who uses the present system in order to assess the weaknesses and any issues that need addressing.
>
> **H** At this stage, it is also worth setting a preliminary timeframe.

TIP
In the Test of Reading, you need to read quickly as well as effectively. Practise regularly to improve your reading speed. Set aside some time every day to focus on it. Think of this as part of your 'fitness campaign' for the exam, like going to the gym every day.

2 Speed reading

The way you approach a text can help you to improve your speed and gain more from your reading. Work with a partner and put the items on this 'speed-reading menu' in the correct order.

> **SPEED-READING MENU**
>
> **A** As you read, focus on groups of words, not individual words.
>
> **B** Before starting to read the text, read the heading.
>
> **C** Read the first and last paragraph to get a feeling for the text.
>
> **D** Read the first sentence of each paragraph (the topic sentence).
>
> **E** Read the task instructions and highlight any key words.
>
> **F** Read the whole text.

© Mike Baldwin / Cornered

www.CartoonStock.com

'The 10-week course costs $600 and takes an hour and a half to complete.'

3 Calculating your speed

Choose a short article from a newspaper, the web or a specialist magazine and read for ten minutes. You should read so that you understand the gist of the text, not necessarily every word. Count the number of words in the text approximately by counting ten lines, averaging the number of words per line, then multiplying by the number of lines in the text. Then divide the number of words by ten to find out your word-per-minute count. You can keep a record of your progress in a speed-reading log like this one.

	WEEK 1	WEEK 2	WEEK 3	WEEK 4
MONDAY	___ wpm	___ wpm	___ wpm	___ wpm
TUESDAY	___ wpm	___ wpm	___ wpm	___ wpm
WEDNESDAY	___ wpm	___ wpm	___ wpm	___ wpm
THURSDAY	___ wpm	___ wpm	___ wpm	___ wpm
FRIDAY	___ wpm	___ wpm	___ wpm	___ wpm
SATURDAY	___ wpm	___ wpm	___ wpm	___ wpm
SUNDAY	___ wpm	___ wpm	___ wpm	___ wpm

4 Speed-reading practice

Read this review of accountancy software and time yourself. Calculate your reading speed (wpm).

Choosing Accounting Software

As an Accounting system provider, we are often asked 'what is the most important feature to look for when evaluating accounting software?' In our opinion, the development capability of the package is the prime feature to consider.

Accounting software publishers generally follow a strategy of producing software that contains all of the most popular and widely used features straight out of the box. These products are designed to meet 80 to 85 per cent of the needs of all businesses; thereafter, the software authors expect customers and their supporting dealers to use the product's in-built development tools to add functionality to the product, thus fulfilling the remainder of the client's needs.

This approach has worked well since the early 1980s when Sage released the first truly amendable system, Sage Sovereign, later to become Line 100. All of the major accounting software publishers now adopt this approach, as it allows their products to have wider appeal across multiple industry sectors.

In the eighties, the most successful accounting software products required the supporting dealer to modify the source code in order to add additional fields, calculations and further functionality. This approach had several drawbacks. Modifying the source code often required many months of programming which carried large cost implications.

Customers who had their source code modified often found that doing so prevented them from upgrading to new versions of the software, as source code changes left no way to upgrade without losing all of the expensive development work.

As publishers released new versions of the accounting software, their customers were unable to upgrade, effectively freezing the functionality of the product. In contrast, today's development tools are easier to use and in most cases they allow the customers to upgrade to new product releases whilst retaining the developed features along the way.

A system's ability to allow development is not just an incidental benefit today, it is part of an overall strategy to deliver solid accounting systems which contain the core features used by most businesses, twinned with development tools that allow developers to tailor the system to meet their client's needs more fully. This approach enables software companies to keep the core accounting system clean and lean and avoids building confusion into the software. If you are in the market for an accounting software solution, you would be wise to evaluate the software's development capabilities before making your selection.

Steve Garrett, Client Account
Manager, Link Systems UK

(400 words approximately)

5 Sentence completion

Read the text in Exercise 4 again and complete these sentences.

1 According to the writer, when selecting software, the key point to consider is _____ .

2 Software authors believe that customers should _____ .

3 Amending the source codes sometimes _____ .

4 Some customers who changed their source code could not _____ .

5 Nowadays, development tools are _____ .

6 Clients need core features combined with _____ .

7 In conclusion, it is a good idea to _____ .

■ Section B **Exam focus**

Summarizing

Re-read the text in Skills Exercise 4 and complete this summary, using one or two words for each gap.

A key feature to **(1)** _____ when choosing accounting software is the **(2)** _____ of the product. Most software packages are **(3)** _____ to meet 80 to 85 per cent of the clients' requirements and come with in-built development tools that allow them to **(4)** _____ the software for their **(5)** _____ . One of the first systems that could be **(6)** _____ was developed by Sage at the beginning of the 1980s, and nowadays major software providers have **(7)** _____ this approach. This means that the publishers' products can be used in a wider range of **(8)** _____ . One problem in the eighties was that in order to add functionality, **(9)** _____ needed to be changed, and this created problems for customers. Amending source codes was **(10)** _____ and created high programming costs. In addition, following changes in the source code, they experienced problems **(11)** _____ software. When publishers produced newer **(12)** _____ of the software, many customers were unable to upgrade them. By comparison, today's development tools are more **(13)** _____ and give users the possibility to **(14)** _____ . The capability of a system to allow development is a good **(15)** _____ to enable businesses to provide sound **(16)** _____ and at the same time to enable developers to cater for their clients' needs. Therefore, it is recommended that companies **(17)** _____ the software's development capacity before selecting it.

LISTENING

■ Section A **Skills**

1 🎧 `13–15` **3.1–3.3 Listening for details**

Listen to three people talking about choosing accountancy software. Which of these words do you hear?

arduous	❑	crucial	❑	simple	❑
basic	❑	detailed	❑	smart	❑
beneficial	❑	difficult	❑	sophisticated	❑
capable	❑	easy	❑	successful	❑
complete	❑	efficient	❑	time-consuming	❑
complicated	❑	essential	❑	unique	❑
comprehensive	❑	ineffective	❑	unsuccessful	❑
cost-effective	❑	limited	❑	user-friendly	❑
critical	❑	panoramic	❑		

2 🎧 `13–15` **3.1–3.3 Listening to opinions**

Listen again and write which speaker (1, 2 or 3) uses each of these phrases.

1 I always think …

2 Personally, …

3 In my opinion, …

4 I'm sure …

5 I believe …

6 I'm not convinced …

7 If you ask me, …

8 I feel …

9 In my view, …

3 🎧 `13–15` **3.1–3.3 Identifying speakers' opinions**

Listen again and choose two sentences (A, B, C or D) which describe each speaker's opinions.

Speaker 1
A Choosing software is complicated.
B Understanding the basic features of software is the most important point.
C The software should be the appropriate size.
D The software should provide comprehensive instructions.

Speaker 2
A Nowadays, price is still the most important point.
B Most software now provides more solutions than mere bookkeeping.
C These days, most software packages can be used for any business.
D Each package has its own special set of solutions.

Speaker 3
A If you choose software carefully, you will be able to adapt it to your needs.
B It is easy to redesign software.
C The process of choosing software will eventually show you how business processes are connected.
D It takes a long time to find the right accounting software.

4 Reading and comparing

Now justify your choices in Exercise 3 by reading the audio transcripts (page 122) and highlighting each speaker's exact words.

■ Section B **Exam focus**

1 **16–18** **3.4–3.6** **Sentence completion**

Listen to three speakers talking about ACCA qualifications and complete these sentences.

Speaker 1

1 After completing the Professional Scheme, you become …
2 It is necessary to complete three years of …
3 The degree is awarded upon completion of …

Speaker 2

4 In Part 3 of the examination, it is essential to …
5 The most recent changes to the syllabus were …
6 The examinations are held …

Speaker 3

7 Many individuals use the CAT qualification as …
8 Recently, the CAT qualification was put on the …
9 Funding is now available for the CAT qualification at …

> **TIP**
> In the Test of Listening test, you should read the questions carefully before you listen to each section.

▶ See **Useful abbreviations**, pages 116–117

2 **Focusing on vocabulary**

With a partner, discuss the meaning of the words and expressions in bold in these sentences.

1 The **IASB** is an independent, privately funded accounting standard-setter based in London.
2 The Institute has the authority to **promulgate** Statements on Auditing Procedure.
3 We have listened to several **heated debates** on how best to conduct accounting studies.
4 It is quite **a tall order** to expect your clients to comprehend accounting ratios.

3 **19** **3.7** **Listening and speaking**

Listen and discuss these questions.

1 What is the next topic?
2 What changes were made in accounting standards from January 1995?
3 How has this development affected companies with shares listed on an EU stock exchange?
4 What two questions does this situation raise?

4 **19** **3.7** **Focus on detail**

Listen again, then complete these sentences.

1 The _____ of accounting standards has been widely discussed in EU circles.
2 Companies are now obliged to use standards _____ by the IASB.
3 Those companies _____ on an EU stock exchange must comply with these standards.
4 The _____ of Europe's financial markets is not an easy task.
5 Many people question why IASB's standards have been _____ instead of others.

■ Section A **Skills**

1 Interview tips

Interviewers use many techniques to find out as much as possible about your personality. Some stick to technical questions about education and experience, whereas others will try to put you on the spot to discover how you react under pressure. Look at these tips and discuss with a partner which are the most difficult for you.

---

1 **Provide informative answers**
Always highlight your experience and skills in your answers.

2 **Sell yourself**
Mention your strengths and good attributes whenever possible.

3 **Turn negative into positive**
Use the interviewer's questions aimed at identifying your weaknesses to show your strengths.

4 **Remain calm**
Do not react to criticism in an emotional way; focus on the job and maintain a professional approach.

---

2 Handling interview questions

With a partner, discuss what would make 'good' answers to these questions.

' It is not every question that deserves an answer.'
Publilius Syrus

1 What interests you most about this job?

2 What are you looking for in your next job?

3 What are your biggest accomplishments?

4 How long have you been looking for another position?

5 Why were you made redundant?

6 How do you handle criticism of your work?

7 Why have you changed jobs so frequently?

8 What can you do for us that someone else cannot do?

9 What would you like to change in your current job?

10 Why do you want to leave your current job?

3 Interviewing the interviewer

At some stage in the interview, you should also get the opportunity to ask the interviewer questions. With a partner, ask and answer questions about these topics.

About the job
- why the job has become vacant
- the key tasks and responsibilities
- challenging or routine aspects
- extra expectations of the firm (e.g. travel)
- training and development opportunities
- details of any bonus schemes

About the company
- structure of the organisation
- success of the organisation
- the company's long-term strategy
- scope for promotion

■ Section B Exam focus

1 Talking about yourself

With a partner, ask and answer these questions.

TIP
In Part 1 of the Test of Speaking, you will spend about a minute (two minutes for two candidates) talking to the examiner.

- What do you do in your free time?
- How do you unwind?
- What kind of sports do you take part in or follow?
- What hobbies have you got?
- Who do you socialise with at the weekend?
- What kind of holidays do you prefer?

2 Key words presentation

TIP
In Part 4 of the exam, you will be given a topic to present to the examiner.

When your trainer starts the clock and names the first speaker, he or she will start talking about the first topic. After three minutes, the trainer will name the next speaker who will move on to the next topic on the list. Remember to expand each topic as much as possible and add additional information or questions.

Bank accounts	Accounting qualifications
Forms of money	Accounting standards
Functions of a central bank	Financial statements
Financial instruments	Fraudulent accounting
Insurance	Types of investments
Mergers	Shareholders
Assets	Financial authorities
Liabilities	Good accountants

EXAM HINTS

DOs

✓ Concentrate on what the examiner and your partner say.

✓ Ask your partner questions when he/she has finished speaking.

✓ Relax and respond naturally to the examiner's questions.

DON'Ts

✗ Don't ask the examiner to give you a word you can't remember or don't know.

✗ Don't stop speaking before until the examiner says 'Thank you.'

✗ Don't interrupt your partner during their long turn; ask questions afterwards.

▶ See **Language bank, Presentations** and **Discussions**, page 118

WRITING

■ Section A   Skills

1 Introduction to letter writing

a What makes a good letter? Choose from this list.

TIP
In the same way as other forms of communication, effective letters should have a clear beginning , middle and end. As business professionals have a great deal of reading matter to process during the day, letters should be clear and to the point.

   1 Has a clear style and is written in simple English.

   2 Contains plenty of technical information and jargon to show your client you are knowledgeable.

   3 Contains accurate information.

   4 Adopts an informal, chatty style to put your client at ease.

   5 Contains a clear statement of purpose.

   6 Is as brief as possible.

   7 Contains a lot of complicated words.

   8 Is grammatically complex.

   9 Is easy to follow.

b What do you think are the most common problems with business letters in general? Discuss with a partner.

2 Useful language for letters

Match the functions (1–8) and the phrases (a–h).

1 Making a personal introduction	a To conclude, we are concerned by the proposals in the draft to extend financial reporting.
2 Confirming details	b I would like to confirm our appointment on Tuesday 15th August in your office.
3 Closing the letter	c Please let me know what would be a suitable time for me to attend an interview.
4 Requesting information	d I have been appointed to replace Ged Rogers, who previously dealt with your audit.
5 Confirming action	e I would be grateful if you could send me the originals of the documents we discussed at our meeting.
6 Requesting an appointment	f I look forward to hearing from you at your earliest convenience.
7 Expressing purpose	g With reference to our recent telephone conversation, I would like to inform you that we have been in touch with your solicitors.
8 Providing a conclusion	h I am writing to enquire about graduate vacancies in your firm.

■ Section B Exam focus

1 Jumbled letter of appointment

Match the phrases in the two lists below (1–10 and a–j) to create a letter of appointment for accounting work.

1 Following our recent discussions with Rick Kline …

2 This letter sets forth our …

3 It is primarily the responsibility of Smart Bag Limited to compile annual financial statements …

4 We will prepare the annual financial statements of Smart Bag Limited …

5 In addition to the services mentioned above, …

6 Except when agreed otherwise, our fees will be billed …

7 Our fees will be calculated …

8 Max and Max Ltd will not be …

9 This letter will be effective for future years …

10 Should the content not correspond with your view of our terms of engagement, …

a … from information provided to us by the owner(s)/partners/members.

b … unless it is terminated, amended or suspended.

c … separately for each main type of work mentioned above.

d … held responsible for any payment to any authority.

e … we are pleased to confirm acceptance of our engagement to provide accounting services.

f … which fairly present the firm's financial position.

g … we will also provide advice on taxation, as agreed.

h … we will gladly discuss this matter further with you.

i … understanding of the terms and objectives of our engagement.

j … on the basis of the time spent on your affairs.

> **EXAM TASK**
> Test of Writing Part 1

2 Letter of introduction

A friend of yours is a not a member of the Institute of Chartered Accountants in England and Wales, but would like to use their library and have access to material on the ICAEW website. Write a letter of introduction.

Points to include:

- State the purpose of your letter
- Introduce the friend or colleague you wish to sponsor
- Include details of the profession of the person, how long you have known him or her, and his/her reliability
- Mention the reasons why the non-member requires access to the library

Finally, include this indemnity statement:
I hereby to undertake to indemnify the Library against any loss or damage resulting from his/her use of the Library facilities under my sponsorship.

> **TIP**
> In Task 1 of the Test of Writing, pay attention to the accuracy of your writing.

Company performance

This unit covers:

TOPICS
- Financial statements
- Company reporting
- Definition of accounting
- Accounts receivable
- Disclosure
- Big Four accounting firms
- Investments
- The balance sheet
- Fund management

SKILLS
- Reading: text completion, word formation, vocabulary building
- Listening: listening for detail, listening and speaking
- Speaking: talking about your work style, presenting financial terms
- Writing: reports: planning your writing, accuracy

READING

■ Section A Skills

TALKING POINT

Discuss these questions with a partner.

1 What is accounting?

2 When did it start?

3 How has accounting changed in modern times?

1 Sentence completion

Read the text and complete it with the words in the box.

assets	bookkeeping	credit	debit	entries	errors	measures
practices	principles	reform	relationships	transactions		

DEFINITION OF ACCOUNTING

Accounting is the measurement of financial (**1**) _____ which are transfers of legal property rights made under contractual (**2**) _____ . Non-financial transactions are specifically excluded due to conservatism and materiality principles. At the core of modern financial accounting is the double-entry (**3**) _____ system. This system involves making at least two (**4**) _____ for every transaction: a (**5**) _____ in one account, and a corresponding (**6**) _____ in another account. Basically, the sum of all debits should always equal the sum of all credits; this provides a simple way to check for (**7**) _____ . This system was first used in medieval Europe; however, claims have been made that the system dates back to Ancient Rome or Greece. According to critics of standard accounting (**8**) _____ , accounting has changed little since. In each generation, accounting (**9**) _____ of some kind has been made in order to try to keep bookkeeping relevant to capital (**10**) _____ or production capacity, but such changes have not altered the basic (**11**) _____ of accounting. In recent times, the divergence of accounting from economic principles has resulted in controversial (**12**) _____ to make financial reports more indicative of economic reality.

---

2 Text completion

a Read this article about investing in BRIC countries in which some sentences are missing. Discuss with a partner what kind of information you would expect to find in each gap.

Example: **(0)** *An introduction to the article or reference to the report?*

TIP
Look carefully at the sentence before and after each gap and consider what kind of information would fit.

Investors should look beyond BRIC countries, says PwC report

(0) *A report published by PricewaterhouseCoopers on Tuesday has suggested that investors need to look beyond the BRICs (Brazil, Russia, India and China) for future growth opportunities.* 'The World in 2050: Beyond the BRICs' report concluded that long-term prospects for China, India and other so-called 'E7' economies (Brazil, Mexico, Russia, Indonesia and Turkey) are still upbeat, but looks for the first time at an additional 13 emerging economies, which the firm argues also have the potential to grow significantly faster than the established Organisation for Economic Co-operation and Development (OECD) countries.

(1) _____ 'The global centre of economic gravity is already shifting to China, India and other large emerging economies, and our analysis suggests that this process has a lot further to run.

(2) _____ India could grow to almost 90% of the size of the USA by 2050. Brazil seems likely to overtake Japan by 2050 to move into fourth place, while Russia, Mexico and Indonesia all have the potential to have economies larger than those of Germany or the UK by the middle of this century. But the fastest mover could be Vietnam, with a potential growth rate of almost 10% per annum in real dollar terms.'

(3) _____ For example, it suggests that Nigeria, while high risk, has the long-term potential to overtake South Africa to be the largest African economy by 2050. **(4)** _____

However, with the possible exception of Vietnam relative to Turkey, the additional analysis does not change the conclusion from earlier PricewaterhouseCoopers research that the E7 will remain the largest emerging economies through to 2050. Mr Hawksworth explained that:

'**(5)** _____ In fact, it should prove to be a boost for them through growing income from exports and overseas investments, even as the OECD share of world GDP declines.'

b Match these sentences and phrases (A–F) with the gaps in the article (1–5). The first one (**0**) is given as an example.

~~**A** A report published by PricewaterhouseCoopers on Tuesday has suggested that investors need to look beyond the BRICs (Brazil, Russia, India and China) for future growth opportunities.~~

B The rapid growth of the emerging economies does not mean the demise of the established OECD economies.

C John Hawksworth, Head of Macroeconomics at PricewaterhouseCoopers LLP, observed that:

D The report also highlights that there are many other alternatives worth considering, depending on the nature of the investment.

E BRIC economies are likely to continue to benefit from superior growth, from globalisation and from being economically 'coupled' with the developed economies.

F The Philippines, Egypt and Bangladesh also have high growth potential, but also high risk levels.

READING

Exam focus

EXAM TASK
Test of Reading Part 2

TIP
In Part 2 of the exam, you are required to complete a text by filling the gaps with the most appropriate word.

1 Selecting the appropriate language

With a partner, look at this text and discuss what kind of word is missing from each sentence. Then complete the gaps in the text. The first one (**0**) is given as an example.

ACCOUNTS RECEIVABLE

Accounts receivable is (**0**) _one_ of a series of accounting transactions dealing with the invoicing of customers (**1**) _____ owe money to a person, company or organization (**2**) _____ services or goods that have been (**3**) _____ to the customer. In most firms, this is usually (**4**) _____ by issuing an invoice and (**5**) _____ it to the customer to be paid within an agreed timeframe and payment (**6**) _____ . One example of a common payment term is 'net 30', meaning payment is due in the amount of the invoice 30 days from the (**7**) _____ of invoice.

While booking a receivable is accomplished by a (**8**) _____ accounting transaction, the process of maintaining and collecting payments on the accounts receivable subsidiary account balances (**9**) _____ be time-consuming. Accounts receivable payments can be received (**10**) _____ to ten to 15 days after the due date has been reached. On a (**11**) _____ balance sheet, accounts receivable is the amount that customers (**12**) _____ to that company. Sometimes referred to as trade receivables, they are (**13**) _____ as current assets.

ACCOUNTING

ACCOUNTS RECEIVABLE

ACCOUNTS DECEIVABLE

www.CartoonStock.com

2 Word formation

Complete these sentences, which describe notes to the financial statements, using the base word at the end of each sentence. The first one (**0**) is given as an example.

0 Notes to the financial statements are ___additional___ notes and information added to the end of financial statements to provide the reader with more information. (ADD)

1 These notes help to clarify the _____ of specific items in the statements, as well as provide a more detailed assessment of a company's financial condition. (COMPUTE)

2 Notes to financial statements can include information on debt, going concern, accounts, contingent _____ , or contextual information explaining the figures. (LIABLE)

3 The notes to the financial statements are also used to explain the method of accounting used to prepare the financial statements, i.e. _____ basis accounting. (ACCRUE)

4 In consolidated financial statements, all _____ should be listed, as well as the amount of ownership that the parent company has in the subsidiary companies. (SUBSIDE)

5 Any items in the financial statements that are valuated by _____ should be contained in the notes. (ESTIMATE)

6 Differences between the amount of an estimate of any items previously _____ and the amount of the actual results should be contained in the notes. (REPORT)

7 Finally, full _____ of the effects of such differences between the estimate and the actual results should be in the note. (DISCLOSE)

3 Vocabulary building

Look at the four descriptions below of financial statements. Substitute the words in bold with similar words from the box.

accrued	collected	condition	covered	dues	expenditure
flow	held	income	monies	snapshot	value

- *The balance sheet*
  This (**1**) **statement** of financial position shows a firm's financial (**2**) **situation** at a specific point in time.

- *The profit and loss account*
  This shows a firm's (**3**) **revenues** and (**4**) **expenses** for a period, the amount of profit that is (**5**) **reinvested** in the firm (or losses to be (**6**) **funded**), dividends paid to the shareholders, the (**7**) **accumulated** net profits from any previous year's trading and tax (**8**) **liabilities**.

- *The cashflow statement*
  This document shows the (**9**) **movement** of (**10**) **funds** for a period of time.

- *The consolidated financial statements*
  These (**11**) **combined** financial statements of a parent company and its subsidiaries, showing assets, liabilities, and net (**12**) **worth** for the whole organisation.

LISTENING

■ Section A **Skills**

1 Vocabulary building

Match words on the left (1–8) with words with similar meanings on the right (a–h).

1	disclosure	**a**	dispensation
2	retain	**b**	keep
3	heated discussions	**c**	reporting
4	mandatory	**d**	fall
5	threshold	**e**	clarity
6	exemption	**f**	starting point
7	transparency	**g**	fierce debates
8	dip	**h**	compulsory

2 🎧 20 4.1 Listening for details

Listen to a report about changes in financial reporting in Singapore. As you listen, write the missing figures to complete the lecture notes on the clipboard below.

> <u>Changes in reporting procedures</u>
> 1 Reports for listed companies – market capitalisation of over S$ ……… .
> 2 ……… % of firms listed on Singapore Exchange
> 3 Companies that pass the S$……… threshold have one year to prepare themselves

3 🎧 20 4.1 Listening and speaking

Read these questions, then listen again. Discuss your answers with a partner.

1 What recommendation was made by the Council on Corporate Disclosure and Governance?
2 What did the Ministry of Finance decide to do?
3 What was effect of this decision in the financial community?
4 What problem does this change create for companies?
5 How did the Ministry of Finance justify their decision?
6 How will these changes affect smaller companies in the future?

■ Section B **Exam focus**

1 🎧 ▸ `21–22` **4.2–4.3** **Listening for detail**

You will hear two different extracts. For questions 1–4, choose the best answer (A, B or C). There are two questions for each extract. Listen to each extract twice.

Extract 1

Listen to a financial analyst talking about the Big Four accounting firms.

1 What were the results for the Big Four in 2007?
  A All four firms had remarkable results, with significant growth in revenue.
  B Revenue growth in all four firms was rather slow.
  C Three of the Big Four had double-digit growth in revenue.

2 What prediction does the speaker make for 2008?
  A Slightly lower growth is expected.
  B PwC will continue to be the biggest accounting firm.
  C The high level of growth in revenue will continue.

Extract 2

Listen to an accountant talking about the audit of the Big Four carried out by the PCAOB.

3 How often are the Big Four inspected by the PCAOB?
  A Every three years   B Once a year   C Twice a year

4 What was the main conclusion of the last report?
  A The Big Four had not collected adequate sound evidence to support the auditors' opinions.
  B The performance of the Big Four was dreadfully disappointing.
  C Many of the opinions presented in the audits of the Big Four reporting were inaccurate.

▶ See **Useful abbreviations**, pages 116–117

> **EXAM TASK**
> Test of Listening Part 3

2 🎧 ▸ `23` **4.4** **Sentence completion**

You will hear the start of a presentation about the performance of fund management in Hong Kong. Complete the sentences using up to three words.
Listen to the recording twice.

SUMMARY – GROWTH IN HK FUND MANAGEMENT

Results

1 In 2005, record growth was achieved, and Hong Kong strengthened its position as a _____ of Asia.

2 The _____ of the combined fund-management business in Hong Kong grew 25% to HK$4,526bn by the end of 2005.

3 Since 2001, assets under management in Hong Kong have _____ .

Reasons

4 The main reasons for such excellent figures are the professionalism, enterprise and hard work of _____ and advisers.

5 In addition, Hong Kong is a _____ to set up a hedge fund.

Regulatory environment

6 Support from lawyers, accountants, custodians and _____ in Hong Kong is also strong.

Total non-REITs assets – HK

7 Almost one-third _____ in Hong Kong and China.

Launch of REIT

8 The _____ of its kind in the world is Link REIT.

9 Total market capitalization of the four REITs was approximately $6.3m, and its _____ was US$47.8m.

> **TIP**
> In Part 3 of the Test of Listening, you will hear the recording twice. This means that if you miss an answer for a question, you should continue with the next question and listen for the missing information when you listen the second time.

> **TIP**
> **Don't** repeat information that is already in the sentences.
> **Do** check that your answers are spelt correctly.

SPEAKING

Skills

1 Small talk

You are visiting a client abroad. It is ten minutes before the start of a meeting with your clients. Introduce yourself to some of the people present and engage in small talk. With a partner, ask and answer questions about:

- his/her journey
- how business is
- how long he/she plans to stay
- his/her home country
- whether he/she is a sports fan
- where he/she is staying
- the weather
- his/her interests/hobbies
- whether he/she will have time for sightseeing
- his/her opinion about a current affair

2 SWOT analysis

a Your client is considering opening in an office one of the countries below. With a partner, do a SWOT analysis of each country using a table like the one below. Give each country a credit rating, based on your opinion of its overall political and economic risk. You must reach agreement with your partner on each point.

	Bulgaria	Tunisia	Vietnam	Chile
S (strengths)				
W (weaknesses)				
O (opportunities)				
T (threats)				
Credit rating Aaa–C *				

* Credit rating bands
Aaa = excellent; Aa = very high; A = high quality; Ba = low grade; B = very speculative; Caa = substantial risk; Ca = very poor quality; C = imminent default or in default

b Prepare a SWOT analysis of your own country to present to other members of your group or class.

See **Language bank, Giving opinions**, page 119

■ Section B **Exam focus**

1 Talking about yourself: your work style

a Look at these eight factors and their associated questions. With a partner, ask and answer the questions.

> **What kind of person are you? What are your priorities at work?**
>
> 1 Working with people
> Are you a 'people person'?
>
> 2 Working with systems, computers or new technologies
> Are you an analytical person?
>
> 3 Being in charge
> Are you an effective manager and problem-solver?
>
> 4 Opportunity to increase or enhance your current skills
> How important is it for you to be able to enhance your skills in this position?
>
> 5 Stress level
> Do you handle stress well? Can you work effectively under pressure?
>
> 6 Employer's management style
> Can you easily adapt your working style to suit that of your employer?
>
> 7 Size of the company
> Do you prefer to work in a large corporate setting?
>
> 8 Location of the company
> Are you willing to relocate or commute to work?

b Decide how important each factor is to you and rate each one on a scale of 1 to 5.

1 = Not important   4 = Very important

2 = Quite important   5 = Most important

3 = Important

2 Discussion

Discuss your answers to Exercise 1 with your partner.

3 One-minute presentation

Ask and answer these review questions about financial performance with a partner. Then choose one of the questions and prepare to give a one-minute presentation about it to the group.

Focus on delivering the presentation very clearly and accurately. Record your presentations and discuss your performance with a partner afterwards.

> **Questions about financial performance**
> ● How would you describe the balance sheet and profit-and-loss account?
> ● What is a statement of accounting policies?
> ● What is the difference between financial accounting and management accounting?
> ● What is an acid test?
> ● What are SSAPS?
> ● What is SOX legislation, and what does it mean for the world of accounting?
> ● Why is the balance sheet important to entrepreneurs?

■ Section A **Skills**

1 Reports: planning your writing

Look at the checklist below. With a partner, discuss which points are important before you start writing, and which you should consider after writing.

- Read the introduction, topic sentences and conclusion.
- Think about what you plan to write.
- Leave the document for a while, then check it again.
- Read your writing and decide how you can shorten it without losing essential information.
- Revise your text.
- List the main points you wish to include.
- Make each point succinctly.
- Check for grammatical errors and do a spell check.
- Make a paragraph plan.
- Choose the most appropriate format.

TIP
Whether you are preparing a short letter or a long and detailed report, all writing must have a clear and logical structure.

2 Topic summaries

Consider your job. Choose three job-specific themes and write sample titles for reports.

■ Section B **Exam focus**

1 Creating your own exam task

With a partner, create your own exam task for Part 2 of the Test of Writing. Your report task should in some way be related to a client's financial performance.

EXAM HINTS

DOs

✓ Organize your ideas and make a plan before you start writing.
✓ Use as wide a range of structures and vocabulary as possible.
✓ Check that you have covered all the content points.

DON'Ts

✗ Don't use too much language from the question.
✗ Don't include irrelevant material.
✗ Don't write much more than the specified word limit.

TIP
In the Test of Writing, pay close attention to accuracy.

2 Accuracy

Complete the letter using the words from the box.

an	at	both	by	for	further	how	in	made	nor
	of	since	such	the	thereby	this	to	with	

Dear Mr Price,

Re: Shared European views on IASCF and IASB

As representatives of preparers, users, auditors and EFRAG, we were grateful for the opportunity to meet (1) _____ you and the other trustees on 22 January to exchange views in order to obtain a better understanding of each other's positions. We appreciated the constructive and fruitful discussion. We summarize (2) _____ this letter the main European concerns expressed in the meeting regarding global, principle-based standards that were shared (3) _____ all European representatives present.

- Our common aim is sustaining the European use of global financial reporting standards, (4) _____ these standards provide the benefits of increasing confidence in financial markets and of facilitating global investments, (5) _____ reducing the cost of capital. We are strongly committed to high-quality, global, principle-based, neutral financial reporting standards.

- A principle-based approach (6) _____ financial reporting means that clear principles designed to serve the public interest underpin a limited volume of application guidance that show (7) _____ those principles should be applied in common situations. This approach promotes consistency and transparency and helps companies, their advisers and auditors to respond appropriately, using professional judgement, to complex situations and new developments in business practice. With (8) _____ a framework, participants in the financial reporting chain should not feel the need for, (9) _____ require the development of, detailed rules which seek to address all the eventualities that may arise in practice. The IASB/FASB convergence project should not lead to (10) _____ increase of rule-based accounting standards.

- We welcome the continuously expressed support by (11) _____ the IASB and the IASCF for principle-based standards. We call on the IASB to set out the main attributes of principle-based standards and to develop and publish (12) _____ comment an illustrative example of a complete principles-based standard with those attributes. (13) _____ would add to the credibility of the Board and give a clear indication to the market of the direction in which the IASB is heading when it expresses its support for principle-based standards. (14) _____ achievement of a principle-based system will need incremental steps by all financial reporting constituents. The IASB has to play a leading role in this respect.

Way forward

We commend the IASCF on the good progress (15) _____ in improving its governance. We welcome the recently announced accelerated review of the IASCF and IASB governance arrangements aimed (16) _____ enhanced public accountability. However, in our view, (17) _____ steps are required, as discussed in this letter, to improve the governance of the IASCF and the responsiveness of the IASB to its constituents. We appreciate the great progress made by the IASB in creating the stable platform of standards and repeat our common aim of sustaining the European use (18) _____ IFRS.

Yours sincerely,

Chairman of EFRAG Supervisory Board

Auditing

This unit covers:

TOPICS
- Auditing reports
- Basic auditing principles
- European and US auditing principles
- Harmonization of financial reporting
- Forensic accounting
- Auditing interviews
- Recruitment of auditors

SKILLS
- Reading: finding the right word, reading topic sentences, scanning a text
- Listening: listening and sequencing, note-taking
- Speaking: presenting a firm, discussing auditing issues
- Writing: writing accurately, presenting arguments

READING

■ Section A Skills

TALKING POINT

Discuss these questions.

1 What is the main priority of an auditor?

2 Why has the auditing profession been criticized in recent years?

> **TIP**
> In Part 2 of the Test of Reading, you have to complete a text in which some of the words have been removed.

1 Finding the right word

In this short description of an auditor's report, some of the nouns are missing. Complete the text, using the words in the column on the right. The first one (**0**) is given as an example.

The auditor's report is a formal opinion, or (**0**) <u>disclaimer</u> thereof, issued by either an internal auditor or an independent external auditor as a (**1**) _____ of an internal or external audit or (**2**) _____ performed on a legal (**3**) _____ or subdivision thereof, referred to as an (**4**) _____ . The report is subsequently provided to a (**5**) _____ , who could be an individual, a group of persons, a company or a (**6**) _____ , in order to make decisions based on the results of the audit.

An auditor's report is considered an essential (**7**) _____ when reporting financial information to users, particularly in (**8**) _____ . Since many third-party users prefer, or even require, financial information to be certified by an independent external auditor, many auditees rely on auditor reports to certify their (**9**) _____ in order to attract (**10**) _____ .

auditee
business
~~disclaimer~~
entity
evaluation
government
information
investors
result
tool
user

> **TIP**
> In the Test of Reading, highlight key words to help you find similar words in the questions and the texts.

2 Pre-reading

Before reading, consider these questions and highlight the key words. Then search the text below for the answers and mark the part in the text which gives you the answer.

1 When did forensic accounting start?

2 What famous gangster was investigated with the use of a forensic accountant?

3 What kind of government institutions use forensic accountants?

4 What does a forensic accountant actually do?

5 What does forensic accounting lack compared to other branches of accounting?

6 When are forensic accountants usually engaged?

3 Reading topic sentences

In this text, the first sentence of each paragraph is missing. Read it, then choose the appropriate topic sentence for each paragraph from the sentences below (A–F). There is one extra sentence which you do not need to use.

What to look for in a forensic accountant
by Thomas Levanti

1 _____ A forensic accountant reviews evidence, conducts analyses, interviews involved parties and draws conclusions. Forensic accountants are usually retained after an alleged fraud has taken place to assess the extent of a fraud and to bring those responsible to justice. Forensic accountants are frequently called upon to provide expert testimony on fraud and accounting-related matters. Forensic accountants can also be used to set up proactive fraud-prevention programs.

2 _____ Al Capone, one of the most famous gangsters of the 20th century, was prosecuted for tax evasion with the use of a forensic accountant by the Internal Revenue Service. Today, forensic accountants in their expanded role can be relied on to work on all types of cases where having knowledge of accounting principles and investigations has been applied to some of the biggest cases ever, including terrorism and corporate fraud cases, especially in light of 9/11 and Enron. A forensic accountant possesses the knowledge and expertise to interpret financial statements or to work under circumstances where financial information has been destroyed or tampered with, necessitating the recreation of information to determine if inappropriate actions have taken place.

3 _____ Many accounting firms, both large and small, have developed forensic accounting practices that serve a wide variety of litigation and investigative needs. Many private investigation firms have forensic accountants on staff. Governmental entities, such as the IRS, Federal Bureau of Investigation and state and local police departments, employ forensic accountants to address law-enforcement needs. Likewise, many large corporations employ forensic accountants to address legal and fraud-related issues internally.

4 _____ The cost of each alternative must be considered carefully, relative to the loss. The duration of the engagement must be factored into the equation as well, to address the cost–benefit considerations.

5 _____ Many professional organizations commingle* forensic accounting along with other titles and specialties involving fraud, auditing, and general accounting. When one chooses a forensic accountant, many considerations must go into selecting the right person for the job. In many cases, experience makes the difference between a good and bad outcome. Unfortunately, forensic accounting currently lacks the standardized methodologies and standardized practices found in many other professions.

'Embezzle is a pretty strong word. Isn't it possible he just forgot where he buried them?'

* associate with

A Where can one find a forensic accountant?

B Forensic accountants can trace their roots back to America's Prohibition days.

C The field of forensic accounting has been around for a while, using other names, such as "financial investigations;" however, only a few professional certifications address forensic accounting specifically.

D Forensic accountants are often requested to attend court proceedings.

E Making the choice of what type and what size of firm to hire requires many considerations.

F A forensic accountant is indeed part investigator, part auditor, part attorney and part accountant.

■ Section B **Exam focus**

1 Speed scanning

Read these topic sentences (A–E). Then scan the draft contract below and match each topic sentence with the appropriate clause (1–5).

A Description of confidentiality agreement

B Supply and return of financial statements and related documentation

C Calculation of annual fees

D Percentage fee of amount received

E Costs related to collection of excess amounts charged due to bank error

DRAFT AUDIT CONTRACT

We hereby instruct GHALC to audit the company's interest charges, tariff charges and facilities in accordance with the following terms and conditions.

1 Audit fees are calculated at £375.00 per annum for the main account. Additional accounts and paying-in stations are calculated at £155.00 per annum each. The total audit fee is indicated below.

2 In addition to the above, a further fee is payable, calculated at 25% of any sum recovered for whatever reason including the return of fees, relating to any period up to and including the final date of the audit period covered by this audit contract.

3 All costs (excluding legal costs if they become necessary) associated with the recovery of overcharges from the lender/bank will be met by GHALC. GHALC will be solely responsible for negotiating the recovery of any overcharges.

4 BCALC agrees to maintain complete confidentiality in all matters, and no contact will be made with the bank/lender without first receiving specific written authorization from the company.

5 The company will supply GHALC with all bank statements, facility and other relevant letters relating to the audit period. (Paying-in books are only necessary if there are substantial cash deposits.) The company will arrange delivery of such documents to GHALC at the address below. Documents will be returned to the company at GHALC's expense when the audit is completed.

VAT is applicable to all fees quoted above.

2 Using link words

Complete the sentences below using the link words in the box.

for instance   furthermore   in accordance with
in addition   subsequently

1 The figures must provide comparisons, _____ industry averages and company targets.

2 Our fees are calculated _____ the rates specified in the contract.

3 _____ to detailing its expenditure requirements, Audit Scotland provided information for the Autumn Budget Revision.

4 Following the audit, KPMG was _____ asked to evaluate the project.

5 _____ , accountancy measurements must be accurate, precise and compatible with national standards.

3 Multiple-choice cloze

Read the following description of auditing. Choose the best word (A, B, C or D) to fill each gap. The first one (**0**) is given as an example.

AUDITING IN BRIEF

Auditing is a related (**0**) _but_ separate discipline to accountancy of which there are two sub-disciplines; internal and external auditing. External auditing is the process (**1**) _____ an external auditor is appointed (**2**) _____ outside the organisation to examine its financial statements and accounting records in (**3**) _____ to ensure that the records show a true and fair (**4**) _____ of the statements and the accountant's compliance to accounting standards (**5**) _____ as Generally Accepted Accounting Principles (GAAP) or International Financial Reporting Standards (IFRS) in all material respects. The auditors of a limited company are (**6**) _____ by the shareholders. Internal auditing aims (**7**) _____ provide information for the management of a business entity, and is (**8**) _____ undertaken by auditors who are employed by the company, and in some (**9**) _____ by consultants or external service providers. The auditor's report is usually (**10**) _____ brief and indicates that the financial statements have been audited and also gives the auditor's (**11**) _____ about them. The report is attached to the main financial statements published by a company as a (**12**) _____ requirement.

0	**A** and	**B** however	**C** but	**D** not
1	**A** in	**B** by	**C** whereby	**D** which
2	**A** by	**B** through	**C** via	**D** from
3	**A** order	**B** case	**C** particular	**D** addition
4	**A** record	**B** view	**C** opinion	**D** report
5	**A** referred	**B** by	**C** called	**D** such
6	**A** specified	**B** employed	**C** appointed	**D** identified
7	**A** at	**B** to	**C** for	**D** on
8	**A** usually	**B** seldom	**C** always	**D** never
9	**A** places	**B** firms	**C** cases	**D** exceptions
10	**A** slightly	**B** remarkably	**C** very	**D** quite
11	**A** report	**B** opinion	**C** assessment	**D** results
12	**A** voluntary	**B** comprehensive	**C** statutory	**D** official

TRIVIA

Leonardo Da Vinci's father and grandfather were accountants and notaries.

LISTENING

■ Section A **Skills**

1 Pre-listening

You are going to hear several accountants talking about auditing interviews. Before you listen, discuss these questions with a partner.

1 What special training do you think an auditor needs in order to conduct successful interviews?

2 What kind of questions should an auditor use in an interview?

3 What should the auditor avoid doing in an auditor interview?

2 Vocabulary building

Match the words and expressions in bold in the sentences below with terms with similar meanings in the box.

classify	expertise	loaded	out of date	proof	run through

1 If you **rehearse** your presentation several times, you will remember what you want to say.

2 You need to provide **evidence** of your expenses with the appropriate receipts.

3 This report presents a very **biased** viewpoint.

4 The procedures described in the manual are now **obsolete**.

5 We usually **categorize** our expenses into several kinds.

6 In the interview, you need to demonstrate your **competence** to lead a team.

3 🎧 ▯ 24–31 5.1–5.8 Listening and sequencing

Listen to several extracts from a presentation about conducting audit interviews. Number the topics below in the same order as you hear them.

A ❑ The planning, preparation and rehearsal of auditor interviews.

B ❑ Biased questions and their effect on the interview.

C ❑ The importance of avoiding biased questions in an interview.

D ❑ It is possible to categorize the questions asked in interviews into two main types.

E ❑ Audit interviews are one of the best methods of getting information via asking questions, assessing the replies and asking further relevant questions.

F ❑ The advantages and disadvantages of open and closed questions.

G ❑ The majority of auditors lack the training required to hold a good interview.

H ❑ The quality of the replies to most questions depend on the kind of question that is asked.

■ Section B Exam focus

1 🎧 (32) 5.9 Listening for detail

You will hear a recruitment specialist talking about the internal recruitment market. As you listen, choose the correct responses (A, B or C).

1 Last year was a successful year for the recruitment market in …
   A the third quarter.   B the first three quarters.   C the final quarter.

2 At the end of the year, the market was …
   A in a state of turmoil.   B rather quiet.   C more dynamic.

3 Which topic will the speaker NOT cover today?
   A Employment figures of auditors
   B The drop in salary increases
   C Highlights of the financial year

4 There was a fall in the recruitment of …
   A Sarbanes-Oxley specialists.   B managers.   C internal auditors.

5 The main redundancies were of …
   A internal auditors.   B IT staff.   C contractors.

6 Employers were recruiting staff with experience in ….
   A financial services and banking.   B the public sector.   C IT audits.

> **TIP**
> In Part 3 of the Test of Listening, the answers to the questions are usually in the same order as they appear in the recording.

2 🎧 (33) 5.10 Note-taking

You have one minute to look at these questions. Listen and make notes using the words you hear. Then compare your answers with a partner.

1 What is often the most difficult aspect of an audit for new auditors?

2 What should an auditor do to collect as much information as possible?

3 How do auditees vary in the interview?

4 What is the most important point regarding the manner of the interview?

5 What mistake does the speaker think many auditors make?

6 What should the auditor do at the beginning of the interview?

7 How does the speaker describe the interview process?

8 What is the central figure in this type of interview?

9 What should the auditor's focus be in the interview?

10 What two kinds of questions does the speaker mention at the end of his presentation?

3 Summarizing

In your own words, write a short summary (100–120 words) about conducting auditor interviews using your answers to Exercise 2.

SPEAKING

■ Section A **Skills**

1 Giving an 'elevator pitch'

Read this description of an 'elevator pitch', then prepare to give a brief introduction of your firm or department.

The expression 'elevator pitch' is used to describe the 60–90 seconds an entrepreneur has to interest a venture capitalist in his or her business idea. It comes from the approximate amount of time they would have if they travelled together in an elevator from the bottom to the top of a building.

The most important point when giving an elevator pitch is that you make your presentation interesting so that it grabs the attention of your audience.

▶ See **Language bank, Describing the activities of your firm/department,** page 120

2 Active listening and speaking

As you listen to your partner's brief introduction, make a note of some follow-up questions.

3 Discussing auditing issues

Read these statements about the harmonization and convergence of financial reporting and auditing standards and discuss them in groups of three.

' The auditor is a watchdog, not a bloodhound.'
Lord Justice Topes

1 The reporting method should not differ depending on country, industry, size of company or any other consideration, and managers should not be permitted choices of reporting methods for similar transactions.

2 The quality of both audit standards and the resulting audits differs substantially worldwide.

3 Investors, companies and markets will benefit from the complete harmonization on a global basis of the differing national and supra-national standards.

4 The costs investors incur to harmonize the various standards so that cross-border comparisons of companies may be made are huge.

5 Auditing should not be standardized.

6 Different local standards for auditing should be accepted.

■ Section B **Exam focus**

1 One-minute presentation

Work in groups of three. Choose one of the topics from the list below which have been covered in this unit and prepare to give a one-minute presentation to the group. In your presentation, emphasize three important points about your topic.

1 The role of the forensic accountant in cases of corporate fraud

2 Dos and donts of auditor interviews

3 A brief introduction to auditing

▶ See **Language bank, Presentations**, page 118

TIP
In Part 1 of the Test of Speaking, you will be given a choice of finance-related topics and asked to talk for one minute about the chosen topic.

2 Presentation feedback

As you listen to other members of the group give their presentations, consider the following points and make notes on both positive aspects and points for improvement.

Accuracy
● How accurate was the presentation?
● What kind of mistakes did you notice?

Clarity
● How clear was the presentation?
● How did the speaker clarify key points?

Speed
● Was the presentation too slow or too fast?

Presence of the speaker
● What impression did the speaker give to the audience?
● Was he/she confident/enthusuastic/calm?

3 Discussing feedback

After the presentations, discuss your feedback and how each group member can improve his/her performance. Make a note of both general points and personal points to improve.

WRITING

■ Section A Skills

1 Writing accurately

In the following article about credit-rating agencies, there are 16 mistakes. With a partner, try to find them.

CREDIT RATING BLUES

Recently, credit-rating agencies sharply criticized for failing to recognie the risks in hundreds of billions worth of mortgage-backed securities which values continue to plummet as home-loan defaults grow. The Treasury, the SEC and several congressional committees are now investigating why credit-rating agencies such as Standard and Poors, Moody's and Fitch gave endorssed securities backed by sub-prime mortgages downgrading them only in July.

Real mystery is why this issue to be investigated. It's obvious why credit-rating agencies didn't blow the whistle. They didn't blow the whistle on Enron on WorldCom before those entities collapsed, either. You see, credit-rating agencies are paid by same institutions that package and sells the securities the agencies are rating. If investment bank doesn't like the rating, it doesn't have to pay it. And even if it likes the rating, they pays only after the security is sold. It's as if movie studios hired film critics to review their movies, and paid them only if the reviews were positive enough to get lots of people to see a movie.

Until the recent colapse, the results was great for credit-rating agencies. Profits at Moody's more than doubled between 2002 and 2006. And it was a great ride for the issuers of mortgage-backed securities. Demand soared due to the high ratings expanded the market. Traders that bought, rebundled and then sold them didn't have to examined anything except the ratings. It was actually a market in credit ratings – a multi-billion-dollar game of musical chairs. Then the music stopped.

---

2 Checking your spelling

This is a list of words that are frequently misspelt. Circle the correct spelling and compare your answers with a partner.

	A	B	C	D
1	A acheve	B acheive	C achieve	D achive
2	A maintaning	B mantaining	C maintianing	D maintaining
3	A interviwed	B interwiewed	C interveiwed	D interviewed
4	A increasingly	B incresingly	C increaseingly	D increasigely
5	A hypophysis	B hypothesees	C hypothesis	D hypophesis
6	A friquently	B frequantly	C frecuently	D frequently
7	A emphasis	B emphasus	C emphisize	D emphisis
8	A diveded	B divided	C devided	D dividid
9	A developpment	B divlement	C development	D divelopement
10	A criticicm	B criticism	C critisism	D critism
11	A choise	B chouce	C choce	D choice
12	A biginning	B beginning	C begining	D begginin

■ Section B Exam focus

1 Presenting arguments

Choose one of the topics below and write a short introductory paragraph to a report which discusses the arguments for and against.

1 Accrual accounting

2 Outsourcing of accounting

3 Harmonizing auditing standards

▶ See **Language bank, Presenting arguments**, page 119

EXAM TASK
Test of Writing Part 2

2 Writing a report

Write a report to a client outlining some of the benefits of establishing an internal auditing department for the management of a medium-sized furniture manufacturer. In your report, you should explain:

- the main function of an internal auditing department
- how internal auditing differs from external auditing
- how the external auditor assesses internal control
- ways in which internal auditing can be beneficial to a company.

▶ See **Language bank, Structuring a composition**, page 120

www.CartoonStock.com

A.BACALL

'I see you have all of your checks and receipts. What are you trying to hide?'

Ethics

This unit covers:

TOPICS
- Accounting ethics
- Ethical reporting principles
- Ethical dilemmas
- Sarbanes-Oxley Act
- Training in ethics for accountants
- Changes to ethics standards
- Accounting abbreviations

SKILLS
- Reading: ordering a text, predicting unknown words, forming words
- Listening: note-taking, speed listening, listening for detail
- Speaking: discussing ethics, answering questions, ending presentations
- Writing: writing an auditor's report, sequencing reports

READING

■ Section A Skills

TALKING POINT

Discuss these questions.

1 What aspects of ethics did you study prior to qualifying?

2 After accounting scandals such as Enron, how can certification programmes be changed to help accountants deal with issues of ethics?

1 Pre-reading

Before reading the text, discuss with a partner the meanings of the words in bold in these sentences.

1 It is crucial to **distinguish** between cash basis and accrual basis of accounting.

2 Most CEOs resist the **temptation** to use their accounting system to misrepresent the results of operations.

3 Here is a list of **ad-hoc** accounting queries.

4 The panel discussed why **consistency** of accounting standards matters.

5 The candidate should have the ability to orally **articulate** audit findings and procedures.

6 Our software helps accountants check the accuracy and completeness of the **underlying** accounting data.

2 Ordering a text

Re-order the paragraphs in this extract from a report about ethical reporting principles so that they read logically.

ETHICAL REPORTING PRINCIPLES

A Finally, it is also important to distinguish what activities are truly voluntary and what are not. For example, there are legal requirements on some industries (notably the telephone, water, gas and electrical sectors) related to providing easy access to services for disabled customers. Despite being excellent work, it would not be appropriate to claim this as part of a voluntary programme covering social responsibility in business.

B Companies should also avoid the temptation to advertise themselves as having solved all their problems. It is far better for a company to commit to continuous improvement in this arena.

C A key test of leadership is the consistency with which the company's different forms of communication reflect the same message.

D This integration of reporting to cover not only financial but also social and environmental issues can permit a 'triple bottom line' form of accounting or a development into 'sustainability reporting' – that is, reporting on all the company's activities in a way that demonstrates its commitment to meeting long-term as well as short-term responsibilities and goals.

E For many companies, the formal Annual Report can act as a spine, containing core messages and articulating central purpose, values and principles. Numerous larger companies already make a point of connecting this with their other communications on social and environmental issues. They thus make it clear that there is a genuine company approach to overall social impact, rather than just a set of ad-hoc initiatives.

F However, it's important not to over-claim. This can create the impression that your work is just a publicity front. Commercial sponsorships, for example, should not be presented as community investments.

G Separate reports on environmental or social impact are therefore valuable, but they need very clear links back to the underlying logic of your business purpose.

3 Vocabulary building

Match the words (1–6) from the text in Exercise 4 with their meanings (a–f).

1 to adhere to		**a** endorse	
2 vigilant		**b** protect	
3 adopt		**c** failure	
4 errant		**d** cautious	
5 safeguard		**e** mistaken	
6 oversight		**f** to comply with	

4 Predicting unknown words

In this extract, some of the words have been replaced by the names of animals. Read the whole article, then look carefully at the words before and after each animal name and try to predict:

- what type of word is missing – verb, noun, adjective, etc.
- the exact word required to complete the gap.

Example: (0) *noun – creditors*

Accounting and professional ethics

Because investors and **(0) horses** place great reliance on financial statements in making their investment and credit **(1) snakes**, it is imperative that the financial reporting process be **(2) tiger** and dependable. Accountants are expected to behave in an entirely **(3) monkey** fashion, and this is generally the case. To help ensure integrity in the reporting process, the profession has adopted a **(4) wolf** of ethics with which its licensed members must **(5) crocodile**. In addition, checks and **(6) foxes** via the audit process, government oversight, and the ever-vigilant 'plaintiff's attorney' all serve a **(7) whale** role in providing additional safeguards against the errant **(8) giraffe**. If you are preparing to enter the accounting profession, you **(9) mouse** do so with the intention of behaving with honour and integrity. If you are not planning to enter the profession, you will likely **(10) bat** upon accountants in some aspect of your personal or professional **(11) elephant**. You have every right to expect those accountants to behave in a completely trustworthy and ethical fashion. After all, you will be **(12) bear** them with your financial resources and confidential information.

■ Section B **Exam focus**

1 Gapped text

For each section of this text (1–6), select the best sentence (A–G) to complete it. Remember to read the sections prior to and after each gap carefully. Discuss your choices with a partner. There is one extra sentence which you do not need to use.

TIP
In Part 5 of the exam, you are required to select the sentences which fit the gaps in a text.

The Ethical Dilemma

Imagine that you are the Chief Financial Officer of a medium to large company. It is April, and the Chief Executive Officer has just returned from a meeting with the company's bankers. She calls you to her office to discuss the results of the negotiations. As things stand, the company requires a fairly significant injection of capital, which will be used to modernize plant and equipment. **(1)** _____

Existing machinery is incapable of manufacturing the required level of quality. Whilst the bank is sympathetic, current lending policies require borrowers to demonstrate an adequate current and projected cashflow, as well as a level of profitability sufficient to indicate a capacity to make repayments from an early date. **(2)** _____ Strictly speaking, the figures would not satisfy the bank's criteria.

The CEO reminds you of all of this and then mentions that she has told the bank that the company is in excellent shape, that she believes that its financial results will meet the criteria and that she will ask the Chief Financial Officer to deliver a financial report to the bank at the beginning of the next week. She tells you that it is up to you to decide upon the contents of that report. Two final pieces of information:

- you have recently purchased a home, leveraged with a significant mortgage;
- failure to invest and gain the promised new orders is almost certain to lead to major retrenchments of personnel.

Let's look at some of the most obvious ethical questions arising in a case such as this:

> Should the accountant tell the truth to the bank, irrespective of the consequences? Does the accountant have a duty to do everything possible to ensure the preservation of jobs at the factory?
> **(3)** _____

Whilst this presentation involves a fictional dilemma, it is not too far removed from the actual experience of many practitioners. Even so, it is important to realize that there is still something rather artificial about such a construction. It's not that the case is unreal. **(4)** _____

Indeed, one of the things that we need to acknowledge is that many people find it difficult to recognize an ethical dilemma as such. It is not that most people are inherently unethical. **(5)** _____

Before trying to explain the reason for this, it may be interesting to pause and consider some of the relatively 'invisible' cases where ethical questions seem to be ignored. Take a simple example: have you ever seen a person avoid taking a telephone call by telling someone else to answer and say that the person is not there? Even such a simple case has at least two aspects to consider. **(6)** _____ Some might respond by saying that this sort of behaviour is quite harmless. But is it really? What sort of message does such behaviour give about the prevailing values of an organization? How easy is it to accept an avowal of honesty from a person who is habitually deceitful for the sake of minor personal convenience?

A Instead, the problem is that many people are unconscious of the fact that nearly everything that they do has an ethical dimension.

B Rather, the problem arises from the fact that most ethical dilemmas are of a much smaller dimension, perhaps lacking the obvious significance of the type of 'big-ticket' issue outlined above.

C The company has been promised new orders if it can produce goods to an international standard.

D Firstly, there is the matter of deceit, and secondly there is the matter of getting someone else to do the 'dirty work'.

E How should the accountant tackle the matter of loyalty to the CEO?

F Practical concerns and pragmatic considerations can make one relatively blind when it comes to spotting ethical issues which arise.

G The problem is that, largely because of some industrial problems, the business has not been performing at a level which realizes even its 'unimproved' potential.

EXAM TASK
Test of Reading Part 3

2 Word formation

Read this introduction to an article about the tightening of reporting regulations. Use the words in the box to the right of the text to form one word that fits in the same numbered gap in the text. For each gap (1–10), write the words in CAPITAL LETTERS.

A crucial test for new CPAs

The number and magnitude of recent business scandals have created an overwhelming need to re-examine the (1) _____ environment of the accounting profession. The confidence in the integrity of financial statements has (2) _____ . Since the downfall of Enron, WorldCom, and others, changes have certainly been made or proposed in an attempt to restore the public's confidence, such as the Sarbanes-Oxley Act of 2002, the most significant accounting (3) _____ since 1933. The act created the Public Company Accounting Oversight Board, which has the authority to set and enforce auditing, (4) _____ , quality control and ethics standards for auditors of public companies. Furthermore, the Act creates new roles for audit committees and auditors, creates tougher (5) _____ for those who commit certain fraudulent acts, and requires (6) _____ of public stock and their auditors to adhere to new rules and procedures for the financial reporting and audit process. For example, managers are now required to assess and make (7) _____ about the effectiveness of the company's internal control structure. The chief executive and chief financial officers must certify the (8) _____ of the company's quarterly and annual reports. Additionally, a new fraud standard has been issued, SAS 99: (9) _____ of Fraud in a Financial Statement Audit, which provides more specific guidance to auditors regarding the (10) _____ of fraud.

1	REGULATE
2	DETERIORATE
3	LEGISLATE
4	ATTEST
5	PENALTY
6	ISSUE
7	REPRESENT
8	ACCURATE
9	CONSIDER
10	DETECT

LISTENING

■ Section A **Skills**

1 Pre-listening

You are going to hear five accounting students discussing changes to the ethics exam. Before you listen, discuss with a partner what the following terms mean.

1 AICPA

2 The Sarbanes-Oxley Act

3 SAS 99

4 CPA

▶ See **Useful abbreviations**, pages 116–117

2 🎧 34–38 **6.1–6.5 Note-taking**

Listen to five students' comments and make notes under these headings.

● Recommendations
● Benefits
● Weaknesses

3 Summarizing

Using your notes from Exercise 2, summarize each speaker's views and recommendations about ethics training.

'I love to come here because it reminds me of how I became a capitalist.'

www.CartoonStock.com

■ Section B Exam focus

1 🎧 💿 **39** **6.6 Speed listening**

You are going to hear 11 abbreviations. Listen and write each abbreviation and what it stands for. Compare your answers with members of the group.

▶ See **Useful abbreviations**, pages 116–117

2 🎧 💿 **40** **6.7 Listening for detail**

Listen to a more detailed explanation of three of the abbreviations from Exercise 1. Take notes, then decide which abbreviations the speaker is talking about.

> **EXAM TASK**
> Test of Listening Part 1

3 🎧 💿 **41–43** **6.8–6.10 Multiple choice**

You will hear three different extracts. There are two questions for each extract. For each question (1–6), mark one letter (A, B or C) for the correct answer. You will hear each extract twice.

Extract 1

You will hear a financial analyst talking on a radio programme.

1 What is going to be the main focus of today's programme?
   A providing some help to avoid being audited by the tax authorities
   B showing you how to keep detailed records
   C providing some figures about IRS audits in 2007

2 What is the speaker's advice about avoiding an audit?
   A Do not put cash in an offshore account.
   B Keep a record of all your previous returns.
   C Maintain detailed records and keep all receipts.

Extract 2

You will hear a teacher talking to a group of pupils.

3 What does the audit assure?
   A that the information on the financial statement is perfect
   B that the statements do not contain misstatements
   C that the financial statements abide by generally acceptable standard and accounting principles

4 How are financial statements regarded to conform to GAAP?
   A if the accounting principles used are consistent
   B if the management generally follows GAAP and generally conforms to its principles
   C if the management adopts accounting principles that are usually applied by the accounting profession

Extract 3

You will hear a news item about protecting the term accountant.

5 What are the main accounting bodies trying to persuade the government to do?
   A to stop accountants without formal education from practising
   B to legally define who is allowed to be described as an accountant
   C to prevent problems with non-qualified accountants

6 What kind of research are the main accounting bodies carrying out?
   A to find out what kind of problems were caused by unqualified accountants
   B to establish the percentage of non-qualified accountants
   C to discover how many members have solved problems due to non-qualified accountants

SPEAKING

■ Section A Skills

1 Ethics quiz

Do this quiz with a partner and discuss your answers.

Ethics quiz

1 Records transfer

A former tax client of yours demands you provide copies of all his records to his new accountant. The former client has not yet paid you for preparing last year's tax returns.

How would you respond to this request?

2 Business valuation

Your client, ABC Pest Control, for whom you've only prepared corporate tax returns, has asked you to perform a business valuation for the purpose of a buy-sell insurance contract for the two stockholders. You have never formally performed a business valuation and possess no ABV or CVA designations.

Would you provide this service to your client?

3 Client confidentiality

You specialize in accounting for fish processors. Your client, Best Fish, requires an audited financial statement. You are currently engaged in an audit of Top Fish, a competitor of Best Fish. In the audit of Top Fish, you learn that a customer of both businesses is about to file for bankruptcy.

Can the CPA perform the audit for both clients, and can the information learned in the Top Fish engagement be used in the Best Fish engagement?

4 Disclosure conflict: business

A general partnership owned by two partners engages you to provide services to the partnership and each of the partners. One partner has a 70% share and the other 30%. Two years into the engagement, the majority partner solicits you to provide confidential advice on how to creatively finance some large debts he has accumulated.

What are the issues in this request?

5 Fiduciary duty

You have been doing tax work for a limited partnership as well as for the general partners of the partnership. After three years, you notice the general partners are paying themselves fees larger than those that were specified in the limited partnership agreement.

How would you address this situation?

'Of course I know the difference between right and wrong! Wrong pays better!'

2 Approaching tricky interview questions

Look at these interview questions. Work with a partner to decide what you think would be a good answer to each question and what would constitute a bad answer (i.e. your potential employer would not like this answer).

1 Don't you think you are overqualified?

2 Do you mind reporting to a boss who is ten years younger than you?

3 What's your biggest weakness?

4 Where do you want to be in five years' time?

5 Who do you admire the most, and why?

6 Describe your current situation and tell me about a significant achievement you are very proud of.

7 Tell me about the longest day you worked at the office last month. When did this happen, and what did you accomplish?

8 Why do you think you are the best person for the job?

9 Tell me about yourself.

10 How did you prepare yourself for this interview?

11 What are your long-term goals?

12 Why did you leave your last job?

■ Section B **Exam focus**

1 Concluding a presentation

At the end of every presentation, you should:

● announce that you are concluding

● summarize the main points

● make a strong final comment

● invite questions politely.

Create a topic for yourself and your partner. Then practise summarizing and concluding your presentations.

▶ See **Language bank, Discussions** and **Presentations**, page 118

> ' If you fail to prepare, you are prepared to fail.'
> **Mark Spitz**

TIP
Remember that rehearsing is an essential part of every presentation; you wouldn't go to the theatre to find that none of the actors had learnt their lines, nor would you be very impressed if the orchestra stopped playing in the middle of a concert because they had forgotten the rest of the music.

2 Three-minute presentation

Prepare to deliver a three-minute presentation to the group in which you present three main points. Choose from this list of topics.

● Three of the most common complaints made against accounting firms

● Three accounting scandals in recent years

● Three problems graduate accountants face

● Three tricky parts of the accounting exam

● Three conflicts of interest an accountant may face

● Three important points to pay attention to in financial statements

Rehearse your presentation with a partner.

▶ See **Language bank, Clarifying and explaining**, page 120

WRITING

■ Section A Skills

Writing an auditor's report

The usual format for an external audit report on the financial statements of a company incorporated in Great Britain is as follows:

1 Opening or introductory paragraph

2 Scope paragraph with respective responsibilities of directors and auditors and basis of opinion

3 Opinion paragraph

Write a short auditor's report of company XYZ, using this framework.

Opening or introductory paragraph (about XYZ)

- Identify the financial statements, including the date and period covered by the financial statements.
- Include a statement that the financial statements are the responsibility of XYZ's management and a statement that the responsibility of the auditor is to express an opinion on the financial statements based on the audit.

Scope paragraph

- Describe the scope of the audit by stating that the audit was conducted in accordance with established standards or practices.
- Include a statement that the audit was planned and performed to obtain reasonable assurance about whether the financial statements are free of material misstatement.
- Describe the audit as including;
  a Examining on a test basis; evidence to support the financial statements and disclosures
  b Assessing the accounting principles used in the preparation of the financial statements
  c Assessing significant estimates made by the management in preparing the financial statements
  d Evaluating the overall financial statement presentation.
- Include a statement by the auditor that the audit provides a reasonable basis for the opinion.

Opinion paragraph

- Indicate the financial reporting framework used.
- State the auditor's opinion as to whether the financial statements give a true and fair view and whether they comply with statutory requirements.

▶ See **Language bank, Linking ideas,** page 119

See **Language bank, Linking ideas,** page 119

TRIVIA

Some of the earliest writing discovered by archaeologists has been found to be records of tax accounting.

■ Section B **Exam focus**

1 Sequencing a report

Below is a jumbled auditor's report containing seven sentences (A–G). Put the sentences in the correct order to form a report containing three paragraphs.

STATUTORY JOINT AUDITORS' REPORT

To the Chairman of the Executive Board of the Central Bank of Tunisia

A The Bank's Executive Board has finalized the annual accounts, and our responsibility is to give an opinion of these accounts based on our audit exercise. Our review has been carried out in accordance with the provisions of article 29 of law No. 58-90 of September 1958 governing the founding and organization of the Central Bank of Tunisia, as modified by law No. 2006-26 of 15 May 2006 and generally accepted auditing standards.

B An audit involves performing procedures to obtain audit evidence about the amounts and disclosures in the financial statements. The procedures selected depend on the auditor's judgement, including the assessment of the risks of material misstatement of the financial statements, whether due to fraud or error.

C In compliance with the assignment entrusted to us by the President of the Republic, we have reviewed the Central Bank of Tunisia's balance sheet and statement of off-balance sheet commitments as of 31 December 2006 and with the statement of the results for the period then ended.

D We believe that the audit evidence we have obtained is sufficient and appropriate to provide a basis for our audit opinion.

E In making those risk assessments, the auditor considers internal control relevant to the entity's preparation and fair presentation of the financial statements in order to design audit procedures that are appropriate in the circumstances, but not for the purpose of expressing an opinion on the effectiveness of the entity's internal control.

F These standards require that we plan and perform the audit to obtain reasonable assurance about whether the financial statements are free of material misstatement.

G An audit also includes evaluating the appropriateness of accounting policies used and the reasonableness of accounting estimates made by management, as well as evaluating the overall presentation of the financial statements.

EXAM TASK
Test of Writing Part 2

2 A brief report

Using these skeleton notes, write an Independent Auditor's Report on Internal Control (200–250 words), in consideration of internal control over financial reporting based on an audit of financial statements and internal control over compliance.

We have audited the financial statements of _____ as of and for the year ended _____

We conducted our audits in accordance with _____

The management of _____ is responsible for _____

Our consideration of internal control over _____

This report is intended solely for _____

Fraud

This unit covers:

TOPICS
- Fraudulent activities in accounting
- Famous fraudsters
- Changes in accounting law
- Corporate fraud
- Forensic accounting investigations
- Tax avoidance

SKILLS
- Reading: sequencing a text, word formation, identifying topic sentences
- Listening: listening for gist, listening and speaking
- Speaking: asking for clarification, presenting and explaining information
- Writing: paraphrasing, writing a short report, reporting results

READING

■ Section A Skills

TALKING POINT

' It is a fraud to borrow what we are unable to pay.'
Pubilius Syrus

Discuss these questions.

1 What are the most talked-about cases of accounting fraud?

2 What effect have they had on the world of accounting?

1 The language of fraud and crime

Match the words and phrases connected to fraud (1–11) with their definitions (a–k).

1	law suit	**a**	judgement made in court that someone is guilty of a crime
2	conviction	**b**	person who has been convicted of a crime
3	to prosecute	**c**	to start legal proceedings against a person
4	court ruling	**d**	case which goes to court
5	felon	**e**	to reverse a decision made in court
6	conspiracy	**f**	blocking the course of justice by refusing to give evidence
7	obstruction of justice	**g**	to apply for a review of a court's decision by a higher legal authority
8	to overturn	**h**	an official decision made in court
9	abatement	**i**	plan by two or more persons to commit a criminal or fraudulent act
10	defendant	**j**	act of annulling a court ruling
11	to appeal	**k**	person against whom a claim or charge is brought in court

'I'm afraid our accountants are being investigated for fraud – on the brighter side, our financial statements have made the *New York Times* best-seller fiction list.'

www.CartoonStock.com

2 Sequencing a text

Put the sections of this article about the Arthur Anderson case in the correct order.

COURT RULING OVERTURNED ON ARTHUR ANDERSEN

A Despite this ruling, it is highly unlikely Andersen will ever return as a viable business. Following its prosecution, the firm lost nearly all its clients.

B From a high of 28,000 employees in the USA and 85,000 worldwide, the firm has been reduced to around 200, most of which are based in Chicago.

C Three years later, on 31 May, 2005, the Supreme Court of the United States unanimously overturned Andersen's conviction as a result of flaws in jury instructions.

D In 2002, the auditing giant Arthur Andersen was convicted of obstruction of justice for shredding documents connected to its audit of Enron.

E Since convicted felons are not permitted to audit public companies, the firm agreed to surrender its licences and its right to practise before the US Securities and Exchange Commission a few months later.

F Several years on, there are still over 100 civil suits pending against Arthur Andersen related to its audits of Enron and other companies. After the prosecution, it began winding down its American operations.

3 Focus on key words

Highlight the key words in these sentences and find the appropriate phrases in Exercise 2 which provide the same information.

1 Andersen was prosecuted for destroying auditing documents.
2 Firms proven guilty of ciminal activities may not operate, hence the firm gave up its operating permits.
3 Due to inconsistencies in jury guidance, the sentence was reversed several years later.
4 It is improbable that Andersen will make a comeback as a workable firm.
5 Numerous legal proceedings continue against Andersen.
6 The size of the firm has been drastically cut.

4 Word formation

Complete these sentences with words formed from those in the box on the right.

1 Ex-Tyco director Frank Walsh pleaded guilty to a _____ charge of taking a $20 million payment.
2 The CFO was charged with fraud and _____ of justice.
3 The firm's former accountant was jailed for _____ to bribe a tax official.
4 Following the investigation, several company directors and senior managers face _____ .
5 In July, a court _____ in Thailand found the wife of the ex-Prime Minister guilty of tax fraud and sentenced her to three years in jail.
6 _____ financial reporting is intentional or reckless acts or omissions that result in misleading financial statements.

| 1 FELON |
| 2 OBSTRUCT |
| 3 CONSPIRE |
| 4 PROSECUTE |
| 5 RULE |
| 6 FRAUD |

■ Section B Exam focus

> **TIP**
> In Part 2 of the Test of Reading, you are asked to complete sentences by forming collocations from a given base word.

1 Word formation

Complete these sentences using the base word in capital letters.

1 The Government has introduced the Tax Laws _____ Bill 2008 to implement a number of improvements to Australia's taxation system. (AMEND)

2 Tax experts can help you to prevent real-estate _____ and other action by the tax authorities. (SEIZE)

3 A client of the bank faces a $250,000 fine for providing _____ documents for a mortgage application. (FRAUD)

4 The CEO was sent to prison for _____ of justice, as he refused to submit his files to the Inland Revenue. (OBSTRUCT)

5 What after-tax return do you expect to get on your _____ ? (INVEST)

6 In 2006, there was a _____ to defraud Kenyans by a cartel called the Kenya Bankers Association. (CONSPIRE)

7 In 1999, Luciano Pavarotti was _____ of tax evasion and had to pay almost £6 million to the Italian government. (CONVICT)

8 The IRS is threatening Nicholas Cage with _____ for using a company he owns to wrongly write off $3.3 million in personal expenses. (PROSECUTE)

9 Individuals who reside outside Norway are only _____ to return to the country 61 days a year. (PERMIT)

10 Audit secrecy in Russia may be _____ if new amendments to Russia's banking law are passed. (ANNUL)

2 Identifying topic sentences

Read the article on the opposite page, then choose the appropriate topic sentence for each paragraph from the sentences (A–G) below. There is one extra sentence which you do not need to use.

A A special audit by Moores Rowland Risk Management later revealed that the company had overstated its revenue from 2004 to 2006 by 622 million ringgit.

B Transmile is just one of several companies now under investigation for financial irregularities, as Malaysia tightens up enforcement against white-collar crime.

C The founder and former chief executive officer of air-cargo carrier Transmile Group Bhd was among three people charged in court on Thursday for their roles in one of Malaysia's biggest accounting fraud cases in recent years.

D Transmile, controlled by Hong Kong-based billionaire Robert Kuok, is the highest-profile casualty among listed Malaysian corporates that have unveiled accounting irregularities.

E All three defendants opted to contest the charges at the Kuala Lumpur Sessions Court and they were released on bail pending a hearing set for January.

F Transmile, whose chairman is former Transport Minister Ling Liong Sik, is controlled by Hong Kong-based Malaysian billionaire Robert Kuok.

G The revelation of the special audit commissioned by the company's major shareholders sent Transmile stock into a tailspin.

H The latest accounting scandals in Southern Bank Bhd and Transmile Group where revenue and profits are falsified through creative accounting indicates three structural failures in regulatory oversight and full disclosure of our capital markets.

Malaysia charges three in Transmile accounting fraud case

1 _____

In a case that has been dubbed Malaysia's Enron, the Securities Commission accused Gan Boon Aun, 46, together with ex-chief financial officer Lo Chok Ping, 38, and ex-executive director Khiudin Mohamed, 50, of having made a 'misleading statement' in the carrier's quarterly report for the financial year ending 31 December 2006. The official news agency Bernama reported that the commission told the court the 'misleading statement' was something that could have induced investors to purchase Transmile shares.

2 _____

They face a minimum fine of one million ringgit ($289,855) and/or up to ten years in jail if convicted.

3 _____

Other shareholders include US-based investment bank JP Morgan Chase and state-owned postal company Pos Malaysia Bhd. The first alarm was raised in May 2007, when Transmile announced that it had failed to meet the deadline to submit audited financial statements for 2006.

4 _____

Transmile had actually made a pretax loss of 172 million ringgit in financial year 2006, instead of the previously reported profit of 207 million ringgit.

5 _____

In the past month, its share price has dropped to more than half of what it was worth a year ago. It closed at 5.75 ringgit on Thursday. A year ago, its share price was around 15 ringgit. The company's shareholders had already formed a committee to take over operations from the previous management. Gan and Khiudin resigned from their top posts last month, though Khiudin's lawyer said his client remains an employee. It is not known when Lo left the firm.

6 _____

Others include Southern Bank Bhd, whose account books were found to have been cooked after it was sold to state-controlled lender Bumiputra-Commerce Holdings Bhd last year.

7 _____

They also highlight the unreliability of financial statements and poor corporate governance in Malaysia,' Lim Guan Eng of the opposition Democratic Action Party said. 'These financial scandals show how poor the climate of accountability in corporate governance in Malaysia is, despite the preventive measures put in place following the Enron and WorldCom financial accounting scandals in the USA many years ago,' he said in a recent statement.

TRIVIA

Al Capone, the famous gangster, was finally sent to jail by forensic accountants for tax evasion.

LISTENING

■ Section A Skills

1 🎧 **44–48** **7.1–7.5** **Listening for gist**

You are going to hear five speakers talking about topics related to fraud. Listen and write the number of the speaker (1–5) next to the topics that he/she talks about (A–K). One of the topics is not covered.

A difficulty finding fraud ❑

B an aspect of fraud you cannot learn on a training course ❑

C ways in which people commit fraud ❑

D statistics on fraud ❑

E the fact that fraud occurs in every firm ❑

F changing records to make figures better ❑

G how you can identify fraud ❑

H the frequency of fraud ❑

I a government report about fraud ❑

J a company questionnaire ❑

K the speaker's views on unmanaged risk ❑

2 🎧 **44–48** **7.1–7.5** **Listening and speaking**

a Listen again and answer these questions.

1 What question does Speaker 1 ask about fraud?

2 According to Speaker 2, who took part in the Ernst and Young survey, and how many respondees had committed a fraudulent act?

3 What three examples of fraud are given by Speaker 3?

4 According to Speaker 4, what is one of the main problems regarding the discovery of fraud?

5 In order to find fraud, what is the basic assumption you should make, according to Speaker 5?

b Compare your answers with a partner.

■ Section B Exam focus

1 Pre-listening

Look at the task in Exercise 2 on page 75. With a partner, spend a few minutes discussing what you would expect to hear in the recording and try to predict what kind of information will be needed to fill the gaps.

EXAM HINTS

DOs

✓ Try to visualize the speaker and the situation.

✓ Imagine the kind of information that may be given.

✓ Predict what kind of language may be used.

DON'Ts

✗ Don't write long answers.

✗ Don't repeat information already on the page.

✗ Don't use words you hear in the recording – try to paraphrase what you hear.

EXAM TASK
Test of Listening Part 3

2 🎧 49 **7.6 Sentence completion**

You will hear a report of a tax-avoidance investigation. Complete the case notes using up to three words in each gap. Listen to the recording twice.

NESS & MURDOCH INVESTIGATIVE ACCOUNTANTS

CASE NOTES   CASE NO/129950: Mr Alain & Mrs Wenche Angelil

Background information

1 The Norwegian owners of the Badenoch Estate, Scotland, are being investigated for _____ in Norway.

2 Mr and Mrs Alain and Wenche Angelil both _____ of remaining in Norway under the tax-free rule for longer than permitted.

Court action

3 The court _____ the couple's summer cabin in Norway for 81.2 million Norwegian Kroner – around £750,000.

Overseas residents

4 In the first three years after registering as resident abroad _____ , an individual is not allowed to stay in Norway over 61 days per year.

5 If an individual returns home and exceeds the permitted period, he/she is _____ to have returned to Norway by the tax authorities.

Fraudulent activities

6 Another investigation of Mr Angelil is pending by the Norwegian Finance Fraud unit regarding _____ of stocks.

Eltek

7 Since its establishment _____ , Eltek has developed into an international company in the telecommunications industry, producing transmission systems and power solutions.

8 The company was listed on the Oslo Stock Exchange in 1998, and was worth more than 4 billion NOK at _____ .

9 Although the company has made _____ of other companies, its value now stands at around 1.3 billion NOK.

10 Nowadays, the Angelil family own _____ of shares in the company.

SPEAKING

■ Section A **Skills**

1 One-minute presentation

In pairs, choose one of these profiles of famous tax-fraud cases each. Read the profile and prepare to present it to your partner.

Lester Piggott

UK jockey

In 1987, former champion jockey Lester Piggott was sentenced to three years' imprisonment after being found guilty of an alleged tax fraud of over £3m. Piggott was jailed after failing to declare income to the Inland Revenue of £3.25m.

The biggest sum on the charge sheet relates to an alleged omission of £1,359,726 from additional riding income. Another charge alleged that for 14 years, from 1971, he omitted income of £1,031,697 from bloodstock operations. Piggott, whose personal fortune is estimated at £20m, is said to have used different names to channel his earnings in secret bank accounts in Switzerland, the Bahamas, Singapore and the Cayman Islands. He was prosecuted in one of the biggest individual income-tax-dodging cases in Britain, and the sentence was at the time the highest to be passed for personal tax fraud. In his day, Lester Piggott won the Epsom Derby nine times and became the youngest ever jockey to win the event in 1954 at the age of 18. He rode to victory 5,300 times in more than 30 countries during his 47 years in the saddle.

Al Capone

US gangster

Al Capone was one of the most famous US gangsters during the time of prohibition in the 1930s. Capone was based in Chicago and was involved in illegal gambling, bootlegging (selling illegal alcohol) and prostitution. After endless detailed investigations, in which Al Capone was famously pursued by federal agent Eliot Ness, he was arrested by US Treasury agents for failure to file an income-tax return. As Capone's testimony regarding his taxes did not match previous statements he had made in a simultaneous court case in Chicago, he was found guilty of tax fraud. In October 1931, he was sentenced to ten years in prison, which he served in a prison in Atlanta, Georgia, and subsequently on Alcatraz Island in California's San Francisco Bay.

2 Asking for clarification and explaining

With a partner, ask and answer quesions about these phrases to clarify their meanings. Explain them in your own words.

1 a volatile market

2 restrictive tax legislation

3 highly exposed investments

4 a reciprocal tax agreement

5 modifications to current reporting standards

6 the company's interim statement

7 compehensive notes to the accounts

8 total cost is amortized in five years

9 the minimum tax threshold

10 profits from subsidiaries are incorporated

11 sceptical lenders

12 non-performing loans

▶ See **Language Bank, Clarifying and explaining**, page 120

■ Section B **Exam focus**

1 50–51 7.7–7.8 **Listening and presenting**

Work in pairs.

TIP
In Part 2 of the Test of Speaking, you have to speak for one minute about a topic and then answer another candidate's question about it.

Student A: Listen to news item 1 (audio 7.7) and report it to your partner in a one-minute talk. After the talk, ask your partner several questions about the news item. Here are some key words to help you.

- bankrupt
- loan
- fraudulent activities
- £10m scam
- hole in accounts
- sale of company
- collapse
- massive losses
- receivership
- arrest

TIP
Remember to smile at your audience before starting your presentation.

Student B: Listen to news item 2 (audio 7.8) and report it to your partner in a one-minute talk. After the talk, ask your partner several questions about the news item. Here are some key words to help you.

- SEC heavy fine
- inflating revenues
- deterrent
- accounting scam
- new management
- manipulating accounts
- mis-statement
- ethics message
- spokesman

▶ See **Useful abbreviations**, pages 116–117

2 One-minute presentation

Prepare another one-minute presentation related to a case of financial fraud and report it to the group.

' A man without a smiling face must not open a shop.'
Chinese proverb

WRITING

■ Section A **Skills**

1 Synonyms

Match the words and phrases in the article (1–12) with their synonyms from the box. The first one (**0**) is given as an example.

0 shows

> comprising   escalation   flagged   incidents   maintained
> professional   ~~shows~~   tendencies   troubles   try   uncover
> victim   watchfulness

UK CORPORATE FRAUD LIKELY TO HIT RECORD HIGH

The latest KPMG Forensic Fraud Barometer **(0) reveals** more than £1bn in fraud claims reached the UK courts in 2007 – the highest since 1995. Government bodies and agencies were the most popular **(1) target** of organized, criminal fraud, **(2) accounting for** £889m of the total. 'Organized gangs have been more active than ever, with a **(3) proliferation** in VAT frauds, ID thefts and other forms of **(4) white-collar** crime,' Hitesh Patel, a KPMG Forensic partner, told the Daily Telegraph. Mr Patel said that, as the economy **(5) weakened**, more employees might **(6) attempt** fraud to improve their own financial **(7) problems**. Increased **(8) vigilance** by companies over unusual spending **(9) patterns** or trends in their accounts was also likely to help **(10) detect** more **(11) cases** of fraud. London **(12) kept** its position from last year as the centre of fraud, accounting for £655m of the £1bn plus in fraud; followed by the Midlands at £117m of the cases; and the North-West, £200m of the total.

2 Paraphrasing

Read the article in Exercise 2 above and paraphrase it in your own words. Start like this:

The most recent edition of the KPMG Forensic Fraud Barometer shows that over a £1bn in fraud claims were made in the UK courts in 2007, representing the highest amount since 1995.

■ Section B **Exam focus**

1 Writing a short report of a case study

Study this report of a case study of fraudulent activities. Then write the report of another case study using the notes on the right.

Case study: Regina vs Mr DBB

The charges

The accused was charged with one count of fraudulent trading contrary to Section 458 of the Companies Act 1985 and one count of forgery contrary to Section 3 of the Forgery and Counterfeiting Act 1981.

Initial assessment

Two meetings were held with the solicitors, in which a review of the documentation and initial assessment of the charges was made. Following these meetings, our assessment letter providing details of our estimated fee for the initial report was drafted.

Initial report

The purpose of this initial report was to identify areas of investigation and to establish whether evidence could be produced to counter the charges. It was also necessary to identify what additional information would be required in this regard. The initial report was based on 834 pages of statements and 6,287 pages of exhibits. The cost of preparing this report was £13,600 plus VAT.

Interim report

This report identified further forensic accountancy work that would be required in addition to that detailed in the initial report. The interim report was based on defence statements provided by the defendant and further unused material in 51 lever-arch files. The cost of this interim report was £18,575 plus VAT.

Case study: Regina vs Mr SC

The charges
- fraudulent trading contrary to Section 458 of the Companies Act 1985

Initial assessment
- one meeting with solicitors – review of documentation – initial assessment of the charges
- assessment – letter + estimated fee for initial report

Initial report
- purpose – identify main areas to investigate – main forensic accounting exercise for interim report – evidence for client's defence/additional defence
- initial report – based on 127 pages of witness statements and 669 pages of exhibits – initial cost £5,800 plus VAT

Interim report
- extensive further forensic work required – additional evidence – statements defendant/witnesses – 33 lever-arch files of financial records
- final report required – estimated costs £25,625 (interim report) and £15,000 plus VAT
- funding approved – initial and interim reports – final report (not yet) – no further work done

2 Reporting the results of a survey

Write a report (200–250 words) about white-collar fraud based on these survey findings.

- Survey based on questionnaires to the top management of 100 medium-sized private companies
- 25% of fraudsters in companies are in mid-management
- Typical fraudster profile: male, 31–40 years old, been in firm five years or more
- Most incidents of fraud not publicized – employees leave 'quietly'
- Management feels fraud risk-management, tighter controls most effective ways of dealing with fraud
- Most companies reported they were able to recover monies lost from 'petty' fraud
- 80% of management believe a whistle-blowing procedure helps to limit cases of fraud

 See **Language bank, Linking ideas**, page 119

Banking

This unit covers:

TOPICS
- Financial reporting of central banks
- Role of banks
- Auditing of banks
- Central bank response to crisis
- The credit crunch
- Banking supervision
- Accounting standards and procedures

SKILLS
- Reading: sequencing a text, matching phrases in a text
- Listening: listening for detail, note-taking, identifying topics and opinions
- Speaking: presenting opinions, discussing banking topics
- Writing: accuracy, writing mini-compositions, reporting results

READING

■ Section A **Skills**

TALKING POINT

Discuss this question.

What kind of challenges do banks face nowadays?

1 Vocabulary guessing

Look at the words and expressions in bold in the article in Exercise 3 (0–12) and match them with their synonyms (a–m). The first one (**0**) is given as an example.

0 b

a justify

b urged

c independence

d refute

e supports

f supposedly

g merged

h rigid

i implied

j inspection

k increased

l turbulence

m restricted

2 Finding details

Scan the sections of the article in Exercise 3 to complete these sentences.

1 Changes in the role and authority of central banks has stimulated requests for higher levels of …

2 Central banks used to be considered to be …

3 Nowadays, the financial reporting of central banks is more carefully …

4 Although many central banks may be formally independent, …

5 With a higher level of independence, central banks are required to …

3 Sequencing a text

Put these paragraphs from an article about the financial reporting of central banks in the correct order.

CENTRAL BANKS IN FOCUS

A Several forces are driving change in central-bank financial reporting, the first of these is the result of significant changes in the role and mandate of central banks. Such changes have **(0) spurred** calls for increased accountability and transparency.

B The driving force of the debate about central-bank financial reporting is the universal adoption of the independent central-banking model. Whereas in the past central banks were seen as merely another simply a part of the government, many have gained significant **(1) autonomy** in the performance of key tasks.

C In this context, transparency cannot be considered to be a burden which central banks bear in return for independence; on the contrary, it **(2) underpins** their independence.

D In recent years, the financial reporting of central banks has become the focus of close **(3) scrutiny**. Previously, the financial reporting arrangements of central banks were almost considered as a secondary issue, but with the financial **(4) turmoil** in recent years central banks now face tough choices regarding sensitive matters such as reserve reporting and dividend policy.

E In spite of these extreme cases, one of the most powerful ways politicians attack the management of a central bank is by accusing it of mismanagement of funds and criticizing its financial statements. The most effective way for central banks to **(5) rebut** this criticism is to find a solid financial reporting framework which protects their independence and thus provides the necessary protection from any criticism that is driven by politics.

F For some central banks, implementing more **(6) stringent** accounting standards may mean that the **(7) implicit** alliance between central banks, government shareholders and other stakeholders needs to be reconsidered.

G For most central banks, achieving 'formal' independence is only the start of a long battle to avoid political influence. Every day, we hear examples of **(8) nominally** independent central banks which find their freedom is constantly **(9) constrained** by politicians. In some cases, Governors have been arrested and even prosecuted or the entire board of directors has been replaced with political delegates.

H Secondly, the safeguards assessment policy introduced by the International Monetary Fund (IMF) has set due diligence standards for central banks of countries borrowing from the fund. Thirdly, the monitoring of how central banks report reserve assets has **(10) heightened** since weaknesses emerged in the Asian financial crisis. And finally, international accounting standards themselves have **(11) converged** and progressed.

I Obviously, this high degree of autonomy raises new considerations. In addition to their more traditional responsibilities for monetary and exchange-rate policy, central banks now have to **(12) account for** their actions and show shareholders that they are operating efficiently and effectively. A key element of this is financial transparency.

■ Section B Exam focus

1 Synonyms

The text below describes the place banks hold in society. Look at the words and expressions in bold in the text (0–12) and match them with their synonyms (a–m). The first one (0) is given as an example.

0 i

a authorities

b confidence

c destroying

d elements

e endangered

f foreigners

g go bankrupt

h key

i ~~occupy~~

j operation

k rescue

l sound

m vital

'If you owe the bank $100, that's your problem. If you owe the bank $100 million, that's the bank's problem.'
John Paul Getty

The role of banks in society

Banks **(0) maintain** a special place in the economic and financial system. Industrial companies may be permitted to **(1) go to the wall** or come under the control of **(2) outsiders**. Banks are usually viewed with a more protective eye by the **(3) regulatory bodies**, although there is no such thing as a complete guarantee of **(4) bailout** for a bank in trouble. Why the special treatment? First, there are not many **(5) aspects** of economic life that can manage without a **(6) secure** banking system. Secondly, banking is a business that depends on **(7) faith**. Allow the confidence to be **(8) jeopardized** and you are a fair way to **(9) wiping out** the banks. Thirdly, banks play an **(10) essential** role in the creation of money; something that governments like to keep within their control. Fourthly, they play a **(11) core** role in the **(12) functioning** of payment systems around the world.

2 Word formation

Complete these sentences with words formed from those in the box on the right.

1 The bank has implemented procedures to help the _____ of accurate information.

2 Strict lending limits should be imposed by _____ bodies having jurisdiction over the lender or borrower.

3 The entire US economy is in _____ as a result of the subprime crisis.

4 Financial analysts warn of imminent _____ within the private equity sector.

5 In future, all credit _____ forms will be carefully scrutinized.

6 As the credit crunch starts to take effect, people are looking for more financial _____ .

1 MAINTAIN
2 REGULATE
3 JEOPARDIZE
4 BANKRUPT
5 AUTHORIZE
6 SECURE

EXAM TASK
Test of Reading Part 5

3 Matching phrases in a text

Complete the gaps in this text about how central banks have responded to recent turmoil in the global market using the phrases below (A–G). There is one extra phrase which you do not need to use.

CENTRAL BANK OPERATIONS IN RESPONSE TO TURMOIL IN GLOBAL MARKETS

Central banks responded to strains in interbank markets **(1)** _____ .
The degree to which central banks adjusted their monetary operations reflected both **(2)** _____ and the design of their pre-existing operational frameworks. Overall, the various actions can be seen as tackling the situation on four fronts. The first response and primary objective of central banks **(3)** _____ through more active reserve management, thus assuring banks of their orderly access to overnight funds. Second, central banks sought to ease pressure in term money markets and repo markets **(4)** _____ expanding, where needed, the range of eligible collateral and counterparties; and increasing the scope of securities lending. Third, central banks increased their co-operative efforts, initially through enhanced communication and collective monitoring of market developments, **(5)** _____ . Finally, in parallel with being more proactive, innovative and cooperative in liquidity management, some central banks also strengthened their monetary policy stance **(6)** _____ .

A the severity of the turmoil in their respective regions

B by increasing the average maturity of refinancing provided to banks;

C although the financial market turmoil had a global reach,

D by adjusting their market operations in a variety of ways.

E was to try to keep short-term money-market rates in line with their policy rates

F to take into account any impact the unfolding credit-market turmoil might have on inflation and real activity

G and later through co-ordinated actions to provide longer-term funds

'The short-term solution is money and the long-term solution more money.'

LISTENING

■ Section A **Skills**

1 Pre-listening

Before listening to a report about the credit crunch, discuss the answers to these questions in pairs.

1 How have banks been affected by the credit crunch?

2 How does this situation affect the auditing of banks?

3 What institution monitors the reporting of banks in the UK?

2 🎧 52 8.1 Completing a report

Listen to the report and complete this summary. The first one (0) is given as an example.

Audit crunch warning for banks

The Financial Reporting Council has warned banks that their balance sheets will be (0) _carefully scrutinized_ in future. The FRC's main concern is that some banks and financial institutions may try (1) _____ the effects of the global credit crunch. The council has also stressed that auditors should be particularly (2) _____ when checking their clients' (3) _____ . Due to the global credit crunch, several large banks have (4) _____ assets and have looked for (5) _____ to cover their (6) _____ . One such bank in the UK, Northern Rock, received a £25bn (7) _____ from the Bank of England. The FRC, responsible for monitoring and (8) _____ the audit industry in the UK, pointed out that the credit-crunch scenario has made the (9) _____ to confidence in corporate reporting much higher than recent years. Increased risks mean that auditors should apply more (10) _____ to the process of checking accounts.

■ Section B **Exam focus**

1 Setting the scene

TIP
In the Test of Listening, you will have a minute in each section to read the questions. Use this time to think about the topics, the speaker and the context.

You are going to listen to a review which provides detailed information about the contents of a financial publication on accounting standards. Discuss these questions with a partner.

1 What do you expect the speaker to say?

2 What kind of language do you expect to hear in the recording?

EXAM TASK
Test of Listening Part 3

2 🎧 🔊 53 **8.2 Sentence completion**

Listen and complete these notes, using up to three words in each gap.

TIP
In Part 3 of the Test of Listening, remember that:
- you should use the exact words that you hear in the recording
- you only copy the missing words onto your answer sheet
- you should check that your answer is spelled correctly.

BOOK REVIEW

Title of book: *Accounting Standards* **(1)** _____
The book provides a **(2)** _____ to equip
accounting and **(3)** _____ with a clear picture of
the complex and **(4)** _____ that apply to banks and
financial institutions. In addition, the book contains several other
(5) _____ .

Two vital features
- The book gives guidance in analyzing a **(6)** _____ ,
  as well as its operations.
- It explains accounting principles that are **(7)** _____ .

Contributors
(8) _____ , such as those working in central banks, as
well as articles and guidance from **(9)** _____
international institutions.

Overall impression
Basically, the book is a **(10)** _____ for those who need
to grasp today's key issues in central-banking reporting.

3 Listening and speaking

With a partner, write a list of questions that will provide the answers for the gaps in the notes in Exercise 2. Then ask and answer your questions with your partner.

4 🎧 🔊 54–56 **8.3–8.5 Identifying topics and opinions**

TIP
In Part 4 of the Test of Listening, you are required to distinguish different speakers and their attitudes or opinions.

Listen to three speakers, all talking about different issues. For each speaker, identify the topic and tick the correct statement (A, B or C) to describe his/her opinion or attitude.

Speaker 1
TOPIC: _____
A There is sufficient evidence to support the view that fair-value accounting produces better valuations. ❏
B The speaker believes that fair-value accounting produces misleading results. ❏
C The speaker does not support the use of fair-value accounting. ❏

Speaker 2
TOPIC: _____
A The speaker is convinced that more compliance professionals are required nowadays. ❏
B The speaker is unsure about expanding her team at this point in time. ❏
C The speaker says that candidates are keen to move to work in multinationals. ❏

Speaker 3
TOPIC: _____
A The speaker thinks that both local companies and multinationals are competing for graduates. ❏
B The speaker thinks a degree in accountancy makes it easier to get a good salary and stable job. ❏
C The speaker thinks that graduates of accounting confront hurdles after completing their studies. ❏

SPEAKING

■ Section A ## Skills

1 Predicting content of a text

a In this text about banking supervision, some of the nouns, adjectives and verbs have been replaced by the names of food items. Read through the text once, focusing on the words in bold. Decide whether a noun, adjective or verb should be used to replace the food item.

Banking supervision

One of a central bank's most important **(0) hot dogs** is the supervision of its domestic banking **(1) doughnuts**. Although central banks are governed by the specific banking **(2) sandwiches** of a country, nowadays many European banks follow directives which are guidelines set by EU laws and **(3) ice creams**. The main **(4) pizza** of banking supervision is to protect **(5) potatoes**. No one may obtain deposits from the public without authorization from the governing central bank in the form of a **(6) fish**. In order for banks to be granted a full banking licence, they must fulfill certain **(7) rice** and pass a number of financial **(8) salads**. The central bank has to be satisfied about the quality and honesty of the **(9) banana** concerned and to determine whether it is professionally credible. The major **(10) cake** for a supervisor is whether the bank is financially sound, and this is sometimes referred to as 'prudential supervision'. In order to obtain authorization, a bank must satisfy the central bank that it has adequate **(11) vegetables**, and a good business plan which has made provisions in its accounts for bad **(12) peaches**.

b Look at the text again with a partner, and compare your answers. Discuss which words would best fit each gap (1–12).

2 One-minute presentation

Prepare to deliver a one-minute presentation of a work-related book you have read recently. In your presentation, include:

● the title of the book

● its main focus

● a summary of the positive points

● what you found useful in the book

● any criticism(s) of the book (if relevant)

■ Section B Exam focus

EXAM TASK
Test of Speaking Part 4

TIP
In Part 4 of the Test of Speaking, you are given some questions related to the task in Part 3 and asked to choose one of them.

1 Giving opinions

Select one of these questions and give your opinion about it. Then ask your partner's views.

1 How far can central banks follow international accounting standards?
2 How should central-bank profits be measured and distributed?
3 What are the implications of IMF standards for central-bank transparency?
4 What should central banks disclose about their reserve-asset portfolios?

2 Three-minute discussion

With a partner, discuss the topics on the discussion sheet. Expand each topic as much as possible and add additional information or questions.

▶ See **Language bank, Discussions,** page 118

AROUND THE WORLD IN EIGHT DAYS

Day 1: Seattle	You are asked to explain to a CEO why the company needs an internal auditing department.
Day 2: Santiago	You are asked to give a brief presentation about forensic accounting.
Day 3: Mexico City	You are asked to give an example of a recent case of accounting fraud in a large international corporation.
Day 4: Kiev	You are asked to explain why central banks should have independence from the government.
Day 5: Dublin	You are asked to explain the main objective of IAS 39.
Day 6: Tokyo	You are asked to explain the role of the Accounting Task Force (ATF) and its mission.
Day 7: Melbourne	You are asked to give a brief explanation of the Sarbanes-Oxley Act of 2002 and its implications.
Day 8: Havana	You are asked to explain how the way banks are audited has been affected by the credit crunch and cases such as the failure of Northern Rock.

TIP
Spend a few minutes reading and preparing each answer. Respond to your partner's comments before giving your own answer.

3 Collaborative task

With a partner, comment on each of these statements.

1 Accountants are to some extent to blame for the recent string of bank failures.
2 The problems at Northern Rock arose due to lax banking supervision.
3 Capital adequacy ratios should be increased to prevent banks over-lending.
4 Governments should tighten legislation and improve consumer education to reduce credit-card debt.

▶ See **Language bank, Giving opinions,** page 119

WRITING

■ Section A Skills

1 Accuracy

Complete the gaps in this letter with the correct article or preposition. The first one **(0)** is given as an example.

---

12 February 2008

Mr Alphonse Dora
43 Oakmount Crescent
London, Ontario
M8V 3O2

BANK
OF
ONTARIO

Dear Mr Dora,

As promised, I am forwarding **(0)** _the_ information you requested regarding confidentiality guidelines of customer information.

1 Banks and building societies will observe a strict duty **(1)** _____ confidentiality about their customers' affairs and will not disclose customers' accounts or their names and addresses to any third party, including other companies in **(2)** _____ same group, other than in exceptional cases permitted **(3)** _____ law or details where disclosure is made at **(4)** _____ request, or **(5)** _____ the consent, of the customer.

2 Banks and building societies will give customers at least 28 days' notice if they intend **(6)** _____ disclose to credit-reference agencies information or undisputed personal debts which are **(7)** _____ default and where no satisfactory proposals **(8)** _____ repayment have been received following **(9)** _____ formal demand.

3 Banks and building societies will at all times comply **(10)** _____ the Data Protection Act when obtaining and processing customers' data. In addition, they will explain **(11)** _____ their customers that they have the right of access to their personal records held **(12)** _____ computer files.

Should you require any further information, please contact us.

Yours sincerely,

Rogerio Florissi
Accounts Manager

---

2 Writing a letter

Write a similar letter in response to a request for information about procedures related to services you provide to a client.

3 Writing mini-compositions

With a partner, discuss these three questions and look at the 'composition menu' on the next page. Then write mini-compositions (50–60 words) for each one.

1 Many local accounting firms are adjusting to the rapid industry changes by merging into larger accounting firms or expanding the services they offer. Does this really assist the clients in the long term?

2 Some finance professionals believe that the harmonization of accounting standards is too costly and that in some countries it would be better to follow national standards. Do you agree?

3 Should central banks really be independent from the government? What are the advantages and disadvantages of their independence?

> **Mini-composition menu**
> - Make an opening comment (do not repeat the words in the question).
> - Make a statement supporting your opinion.
> - Provide an alternative point of view.
> - Conclude your argument.

▶ See **Language bank, Structuring a composition,** page 120

■ Section B Exam focus

1 Reporting the results of a survey

Read the results of this survey on businesses' role in protecting the environment and write a short summary of the results.

Survey results

1 *Do you believe you understand the term 'carbon footprint'?*
   Yes 83%   No 17%

2 *Has your business taken any steps towards reducing its carbon footprint?*
   Yes 55%   No 45%

3 *How important is businesses' role in reducing the impact of climate change?*
   Very important 57%
   Quite important 33%
   Not very important 7%
   Not at all important 3%

4 *How highly do you believe your customers or clients rank environmental issues on the scale of importance?*
   Very important 9%
   Quite important 45%
   Not very important 42%
   Not at all important 4%

5 *Do you believe that the government should force businesses to make their processes more environmentally friendly?*
   Yes 70%   No 30%

EXAM TASK
Test of Writing Part 2

2 Writing a report

You work for an accountancy firm, and one of your clients is a fruit-juice producer. During the last five years, the company's income has grown steadily, and for the last two years, sales have increased by 100%. However, the company has experienced problems processing orders on time due to the low capacity of its bottling machinery, which is now rather old and prone to breakdowns.

The company is considering expanding and plans to apply to the bank for a loan to purchase new equipment which will make bottling operations quicker and enable the company to triple production. As this is a small family firm, the shareholders are wary of taking on the risk of such a loan.

Write a report (200–250 words) to the shareholders:

- explaining what financial documents the company should present to the bank
- summarizing the company's current financial position
- outlining why the company is in a good position to take on such a loan
- explaining why you think the bank would view the company's financial position favourably

Insurance

This unit covers:

TOPICS
- Common insurance terms
- Insurance contracts
- Reinsurance
- General principles of insurance accounting
- International financial reporting standard for insurance contracts
- Captive insurance companies
- Financial stability of the insurance industry
- The regulatory framework of insurance

SKILLS
- Reading: sequencing a text, word formation, completing a text
- Listening: listening for implied meaning, identifying opinions, note-taking
- Speaking: discussing insurance scenarios, reporting insurance news
- Writing: writing emphatically, persuasive letters, linking sentences

READING

■ Section A Skills

TALKING POINT

Discuss this question.

What is the role of accountants in insurance claims?

1 Common insurance terms

Match these insurance terms (1–12) with their definitions (a–l). Compare your answers with a partner.

1	actuary	**a**	attempt by the insurer to prevent the lapse of a policy
2	aggregate limit	**b**	person who investigates and settles losses for an insurance firm
3	premium	**c**	deliberate failure of an applicant for insurance to reveal a material fact to the insurer
4	adjuster	**d**	insuring of risk by one insurance company with another
5	conservation	**e**	person who calculates risks for insurance companies
6	actuarially fair	**f**	limit in an insurance policy stipulating the most it will pay for all covered losses sustained during a specified period of time, usually one year
7	reinsurance	**g**	policy designed to provide coverage under a single limit for two or more items (e.g. building and/or contents)
8	blanket insurance	**h**	replacement cost of property damaged or destroyed at the time of loss, with a deduction for depreciation
9	concealment	**i**	all-inclusive; insurance which provides complete protection
10	public liability	**j**	responsibility of a firm for damage caused to a member of the public
11	Actual Cash Value (ACV)	**k**	payment, usually monthly/yearly etc., for an insurance policy
12	comprehensive	**l**	price for insurance which exactly represents the expected losses

> 'The big print giveth and the small print taketh away.'
> **Tom Waits**

2 Insurance contracts

Complete the description below of some basic concepts in insurance using the correct form of the words in the box.

concealed	confidence	disclose	insurance	judge
	loss	premium	risk	

Fundamentals of insurance

A contract of **(1)** _____ contained in a fire, marine, burglary or any other policy (excepting life assurance and personal accident and sickness insurance) is a contract of indemnity. This means that the insured, in case of **(2)** _____ against which the policy has been issued, shall be fully indemnified. Since insurance shifts risk from one party to another, it is essential that there must be utmost good faith and mutual **(3)** _____ between the insured and the insurer. The insured is duty bound to **(4)** _____ accurately all material facts to the insurer, and nothing should be withheld or **(5)** _____ . It is only when the insurer knows the whole truth that he is in a position to **(6)** _____ (a) whether he should accept the **(7)** _____ and (b) what **(8)** _____ he should charge.

3 Sequencing a text

Put these sentences in the correct order to form a description of reinsurance. Use the words in bold to help you. There is one extra sentence which you do not need to use.

A **Hence**, the reinsurers are liable to pay the amount to the original insurer only if the latter has paid to the insured.

B **In such cases**, in order to safeguard his/her own interest, he/she may insure the same risk, either wholly or partially, with other insurers, thereby spreading the risk.

C Re-insurance can be resorted to in all kinds of insurance, and a contract of reinsurance is also a contract of indemnity.

D Re-insurance is subject to all the conditions in the original policy, and the reinsurer is entitled to all the benefits which the original insurer is entitled to under the policy.

E **However**, if a profitable proposal comes his/her way, he/she may insure it, even if the risk involved is beyond his/her capacity.

F **First and foremost**, every insurer has a limit to the amount of risk he/she can undertake.

G This is called 'reinsurance'.

■ Section B Exam focus

1 Word formation

Complete this description of the general principles of insurance accounting using the correct form of the given base word.

GIM2080 General principles of insurance accounting

The Insurance Accounts Directive (IAD) does not (1) _____ a different set of standards for insurance companies as compared to other (2) _____ , but aims to deal with items (3) _____ to insurers. It lays down a standard (4) _____ for the accounts of insurance companies and specifies the content of items for (5) _____ on the balance sheet and in the profit-and-loss account. Accounts of companies (6) _____ outside the EU will reflect the home state's own accounting (7) _____ . The following description is based on UK (8) _____ .

1 ESTABLISH
2 UNDERTAKE
3 SPECIFY
4 FORM
5 DISCLOSE
6 BASE
7 CONVENE
8 PRACTICE

2 Completing a text

The two texts below and on the opposite page both focus on accounting for insurance. For each one, first select the appropriate title (A, B or C) and then place the missing sentences (D–F) in the correct gaps.

Text 1 _____

(1) _____ This is the second phase of the insurance contracts project, which in 2005 introduced IFRS 4, the International Financial Reporting Standard for Insurance Contracts.

(2) _____ Subsequent editions will address the other principal topics covered. We hope you find it useful and informative and would encourage insurers to provide practical observations and comments to the Board by the 16 November 2007. An Exposure Draft (ED) is expected to be issued in late 2008, with the final standard on accounting for insurance contracts in place during 2010.

(3) _____ Phase I of the project (IFRS 4) provides a specific definition of an insurance contract, temporary dispensations from certain standards, and guidance on implementing current standards not covered by the dispensations. IFRS 4 was designed to enable insurance companies to report under IFRS by 2005. Phase II of the project is the introduction of a comprehensive IFRS, dealing with the recognition and measurement of insurance contracts.

Titles

A Phase II of IFRS for insurance contracts

B Summary of IFRS 4

C International Financial Reporting Standards

Missing sentences

D This special edition of the *Insurance Market Update*, prepared by our Insurance Centre of Excellence, summarizes and comments on the measurement issues raised in the discussion paper.

E The IASB insurance project aims to establish a common standard for financial reporting of insurance contracts, based on a form of 'fair value'.

F On 3 May 2007, the International Accounting Standards Board released for comment a discussion paper on accounting for insurance and reinsurance contracts entitled 'Preliminary Views on Insurance Contracts'.

Text 2 _____

A captive insurance company is defined as 'a closely held insurance company whose insurance business is primarily supplied by and controlled by its owners, and in which the original insureds are the principal beneficiaries'. **(1)** _____ What is the point of a captive? Major Fortune 500 corporations (e.g. Coca-Cola or Boeing) will set up a captive of their own in order to better control, and minimize, their own insurance bill. In this way, they hope to reduce costs from insurance claims, by adopting a rigorous vetting procedure on all claims, as well as gain access to the reinsurance market at better premium rates. **(2)** _____ It is a huge financial market: globally, captives generate $18 billion in annual premium. Their capital and surplus amount to $45 billion, and they control investment assets of more than $100 billion. Captive insurance and reinsurance companies are an integral part of the alternative risk transfer market, which accounts for approximately 30% of global commercial premium. **(3)** _____

Titles

A Problems in global insurance

B Decline in the captives market

C The role of captives

Missing sentences

D A total of 4,000 captives serve their parents' risk financing needs around the world, and this number is growing steadily, in Bermuda and other leading offshore financial centres in the Caribbean, such as Grand Cayman and the BVI.

E In layman's terms, a captive is an insurance company formed exclusively to insure (or reinsure) the insurance risks of its parent corporation.

F In addition, they have the option to decide for themselves where to invest the premium dollars passed down to the captive entity, thereby possibly avoiding third-party investment management fees.

LISTENING

■ Section A Skills

1 Pre-listening

Discuss these questions with a partner.

1 What is 'fair-value accounting'?
2 Why is supervision of the insurance industry important?

2 🎧 57 9.1 Listening for implied meaning

Listen to the introduction of a presentation about the importance of financial stability of the insurance industry. Tick the sentences that are true.

1 The speaker feels that there is a lack of clear distinction between insurance and other financial institutions. ❏
2 The speaker is not sure whether a higher degree of transparency is required. ❏
3 The speaker does not feel that fair-value accounting will clarify the way insurers redistribute risk. ❏
4 The speaker believes that stricter supervision of financial risk are more disclosure are needed. ❏
5 The speaker does not think that fair-value accounting can enhance the way risks are priced. ❏
6 The speaker believes that a more middle-of-the-road approach could help to resolve some of the problems of fair-value accounting. ❏
7 The speaker feels that the discussions regarding fair-value accounting are too emotional. ❏

3 🎧 57 9.1 Identifying opinions

Listen again and, for each true statement in Exercise 2, write the words the speaker uses to express his point of view.

4 🎧 58 9.2 Listening and speaking

a You are going to hear Gary Strohm, the founding partner of an accountancy firm, talking about how the firm started. Before you listen, read these questions.

1 What was Gary Strohm doing six years ago?
2 What did Strohm feel about the clients' needs at that time?
3 What did Strohm and his partner do?
4 What is the current size of the firm?
5 What risk did Strohm and his partner take?
6 What kind of services does Strohm Ballweg LLP offer?

b Listen and make notes to answer the questions. Then compare your answers with a partner by asking and answering the questions.

■ Section B **Exam focus**

1 Key vocabulary

Look at these sentences and discuss the meaning of the words in bold with a partner.

1 The lines continue to **blur** between accounting, financial, insurance and other service firms.

2 Recent articles in the press about the need for consistency in accounts have **heightened** public awareness.

3 A former finance employee at the Hillside firm claims that a **systemic** accounting fraud occurred at the company.

4 **Risk-pool** insurance generally costs more than regular individual insurance.

5 The practice of using credit information in insurance has generated **vigorous debate** among insurance companies, agents, legislators and regulators.

6 The general public have an **entrenched** impression that insurance fraud is common.

EXAM TASK
Test of Listening Part 3

2 🎧 🎧 59 9.3 **Sentence completion**

You are going to listen to someone giving a presentation about the regulatory framework of insurance in the UK. As you listen, complete the sentences using up to three words in each gap. Use the words you hear on the recording.

SUPERVISION

1 The state maintains _____ over insurance compared to some other financial services.

2 The main function of insurance is the _____ from the policyholder to the insurer.

3 Although a company may be _____ when the premium is received, the scenario may have changed by the time a claim is made.

REGULATORY LEGISLATION

4 The first aim of the legislation of insurance is to prevent insurers having problems by stipulating authorization, solvency and

_____ .

5 The second aim of legislation is to provide a mechanism for the policyholders of insolvent insurance companies to be covered by means of a _____ .

SUPERVISORY BODY IN THE UK

6 Prior to 1997, the Department of Trade and Industry was responsible for supervising the _____ .

7 After that, supervisory powers were assigned to the _____ .

8 In 2001, _____ for regulation was taken on by the Financial Services Authority.

SPEAKING

■ Section A **Skills**

1 Insurance scenarios

With a partner, discuss these situations and report your views to the group.

> **I** You are in a meeting with the owner of a skiing chalet which was damaged by fire last week. As a result of damage caused by the fire, the chalet will be closed for a month. Explain briefly how you (as a forensic accountant) can help in the insurance-claim process for both the damage caused by the fire, as well as the loss of revenue for the business interruption claim.

> **2** You are in a meeting with the owner of a hotel that was destroyed by a hurricane. The insurance company has requested financial records to substantiate the business-loss claims. You have been asked what kind of records are required to be able to recreate the company's financial picture and how you can assist in this situation.

> **3** You are in a meeting with a frozen-pizza producer that has had a batch of its products recalled due to contamination. Explain what role your firm of forensic accountants can take on in such a case and how you can work with the insurance company.

> **4** Due to a six-month delay in a construction project, the anticipated commencement date of commercial operations of an insured property is pushed back. The owner of the company plans to file a claim for lost profits and asks you how you can assist him/her in this process.

2 Insurance quiz

With a partner, do this short quiz about the history of insurance.

1 Where were the first methods of transferring or distributing risk practised?
   a India
   b China
   c Iran

2 Who were the first to insure their people?
   a Egyptian pharoahs
   b Otoman sultans
   c Achaemenian monarchs

3 The merchants of which island invented the concept of the general average?
   a Rhodes
   b Corsica
   c Sicily

4 Which culture first introduced the origins of health and life insurance by establishing benevolent societies to care for families of members upon their death?
   a the Babylonians
   b the Greeks
   c the Egyptians

5 Where were separate insurance contracts invented?
   a Rome
   b Genoa
   c Venice

6 How did Lloyds of London start?
   a as a bar
   b as a coffee shop
   c as an office for shipping news

7 What disaster was the catalyst for creating property insurance as we know it today?
   a the First World War
   b the Black Death
   c the Great Fire of London

8 Who helped to popularize and standardize insurance in the USA?
   a Benjamin Franklin
   b Mark Twain
   c Henry Ford

9 The word insurance is derived from the Latin word for ...
   a 'security'
   b 'guarantee'
   c 'protection'

■ Section B Exam focus

1 Reporting insurance news

Read these items of insurance news and explain the main points to your partner.

1

> Fraud is a rapidly growing problem for UK businesses. In the decade up to 2002, the number of fraud cases each year averaged about 60. By 2006, there were around 280 cases; between January and June 2007, more than 100 fraud cases worth $1.19 bn reached court in the UK.

2

> Serious fraudsters are continuing to get away with insurance fraud, as many in the industry focus on detecting the less-complicated claims, such as motor fraud carried out by newcomers to the world of crime. Bogus and inflated insurance claims cost over £1.6 billion a year. This adds 5% to the premiums paid by honest policyholders.

3

> Business-interruption coverage only goes so far in protecting a company from catastrophic losses, and risk managers should consider additional insurance to cover serious disruptions in their business. To complement business coverage, companies should consider insurance for supply-chain problems.

4

> UK-based Direct Line Travel Insurance reported that almost eight million holiday-makers have tried to make a bogus claim on their travel insurance. A recent survey revealed that 15% of respondents had made a fraudulent claim. The fraud is often in the form of extra items being added to a genuine claim, or inflating the value of a lost item. The main item which repondents admitted lying about was sunglasses – the survey showed that 27% of respondents had doubled the cost in their claim.

5

> E-sure, the online provider of home insurance, has noted a new trend in claims involving kitchen accidents. After a surge of programmes by celebrity chefs, the blow torch has replaced the potato masher in the kitchen, but amateur chefs have been getting into trouble. According to the research, 14% of those questioned had experienced an accident or damaged their kitchen in some way while trying out new recipes. Only 30% of those questioned said they had a fire extinguisher or fire blanket in the kitchen. E-sure estimates that £5 billion of household damage has been caused as a result.

6

> *Induced motor accidents are an example of organized insurance fraud, whereby an innocent motorist is induced to crash into the back of the fraudster's vehicle. Claims are made to the innocent motorist's insurer, often including several accounts of fictitious injuries from gang members. Other examples include fraudulent arson, fraudulent disability claims and supplier fraud, where insurers receive bills for work that have been exaggerated or not done. In many cases, these criminal gangs have bogus claims running with numerous insurers at one time.*

2 Collaborative task

Discuss this question with a partner.

Is fair-view accounting really fair?

 See **Language bank, Giving opinions,** page 119

WRITING

■ Section A **Skills**

1 Writing emphatic sentences

Look at the phrases in bold for expressing yourself emphatically, then match the two halves of sentences to make sentences.

1 We **categorically deny** …	a … to change your accounting software.
2 I **deeply regret** …	b … Mr Tide's opinion of the audit.
3 I **enthusiastically endorse** …	c … current difficulties in this market.
4 We **freely appreciate** the …	d … firm's excellent track record.
5 I **fully recognize** …	e … any involvement in fraudulent activities.
6 They **totally reject** …	f … your application was not successful on this occasion.
7 We'd like to **positively encourage** you …	g … you discuss your case with a forensic accountant.
8 Our company **readily endorses** the …	h … your decision to get a second opinion.
9 I **sincerely hope** …	i … you are able to find a suitable position soon.
10 I'd like to **strongly recommend** …	j … any compromise in these negotiations.

2 Writing a persuasive letter

Write a letter (120–180 words) supporting your application to work for a team of forensic accountants specializing in insurance claims. Use this information in your letter.

QUALIFICATIONS & EXPERIENCE
- qualified Chartered Accountant and loss adjuster
- 15 years' experience in chartered accountancy and loss adjustment
- specializes in business interruption and credit loss

MAJOR ASSIGNMENTS
Business-interruption claims
- Global logistics business on presentation of its business-interruption claim following the destruction of main warehouse holding customer goods (£2 million)
- Manufacturer of surgical products following an explosion at plant in Ireland (£1 million)

Advice on loss mitigation and presentation of advance loss-of-profits claim
- Oil company following multi-million-dollar cyclone damage to new refinery in India while under construction ($100 million)

Forensic accounting
- Appointed as expert by a global credit insurer to carry out forensic investigation into an adjustment of major losses.

▶ See **Language bank, Expressing yourself emphatically,** page 120

■ Section B **Exam focus**

1 Linking sentences

Link the following pairs of sentences from the Statement of Recommended Practice on Accounting for Insurance Business using the appropriate link words from the box.

for this reason	**in accordance with**	**in addition**	**in consequence**
	in particular	**notwithstanding**	

1 A Section A lays down general accounting principles in relation to insurers' financial statements.

  B _____ , paragraph 15 requires accounting policies to be applied consistently within the same accounts and from one financial year to another.

2 A In all cases, there should be consistent treatment between the recognition of the claim in the technical account for long-term business and the calculation of the long-term business provision.

  B _____ Note 21 to the balance sheet format, provision for claims incurred but not reported (IBNR), including related claims handling expenses, should be included within balance sheet liabilities item C2(a).

3 A Under these regulations, the old Schedule 9A to the CA85 was replaced by a new Schedule 9A.

  B _____ , the disclosure exemptions available to insurers in the old Schedule 9A have been withdrawn.

4 A It is envisaged that insurers will not normally enter into joint arrangements that are not an entity.

  B _____ , no guidance is given in this Statement on the appropriate accounting treatment.

5 A Provisions, contingent liabilities and contingent assets arising from insurance contracts with policyholders are exempt from the requirements of FRS12.

  B _____ this, however, insurers should apply the principles of paragraph 91 of FRS12 in certain circumstances.

6 A The purpose of this section is to give guidance on the disclosure of uncertainties and estimation techniques required by FRS18 (Accounting policies).

  B _____ , it introduces the requirement to give disclosure on contingent liabilities arising from insurance contracts in certain circumstances.

2 Accuracy with articles

Read this text and add or delete the articles as appropriate.

> The research by Association of British Insurers has shown that the UK insurance companies have paid up £5.5bn in the tax to the government. The group's members paid £3.1bn in a taxes for 2006–2007, ranking it as third-highest amount of corporation tax of any sector. Besides the corporation tax, insurance providers collected additional £3.4bn in tax on behalf of government through taxes such as the PAYE, employee National Insurance (NI) and Insurance Premium Tax (IPT). Data is the first-ever breakdown of insurance industry's contribution to the Treasury. It takes into account all direct and indirect taxes, as well as an employment and environment taxes. Spokesman from ABI commented that these results highlighted success of the industry.

TIP
In the Test of Writing, candidates often make careless mistakes with articles (*a*, *an*, *the*). It is important that you check these before submitting your work.

10 Bankruptcy

This unit covers:

TOPICS
- Language of bankruptcy
- The WorldCom bankruptcy
- The bankruptcy process
- Crisis in corporate government
- Role of insolvency practitioners
- Debt management
- Alternatives to bankruptcy

SKILLS
- Reading: guessing meaning, predicting content, matching missing sentences
- Listening: listening for detail, listening to identify topics
- Speaking: talking about insolvency, bankruptcy presentations
- Writing: sequencing sentences in letters, word formation

READING

■ Section A Skills

TALKING POINT

Discuss these questions.
1 What are the advantages of going bankrupt?
2 What is a debt-management plan?

' Failure is the opportunity to begin again, more intelligently.'
Henry Ford

1 The language of bankruptcy
Match these words and expressions connected to bankruptcy (1–10) with their appropriate definitions (a–j).

1	voluntary liquidation	a	the value of a company in a liquidation as an ongoing entity, which means the business continues, and a higher price is obtained
2	apparent insolvency	b	formal demand by a creditor giving a person 21 days to repay a debt.
3	going concern	c	the placing of a company into liquidation by resolution of its members
4	winding up	d	legal term that means someone is unable to pay their debts and that at least one of the creditors has taken legal action against him/her
5	statement of affairs	e	legal term for a formal application to the court for bankruptcy
6	receiving order	f	person who administers the bankruptcy (can be either the accountant in bankruptcy or a private insolvency practitioner)
7	petition	g	procedure whereby the assets of companies and partnerships are gathered in and liquidated
8	statutory demand	h	document completed by a bankrupt, company officer or director, which gives details of assets, debts and creditors
9	trustee	i	someone who has priority when funds are distributed by a liquidator, administrative receiver or trustee in bankruptcy
10	preferential creditor	j	court order in England or Wales placing assets under control of an Official Receiver

2 Pre-reading

Scan the first paragraph of the article to find the following information.

1 Cynthia Cooper's position at WorldCom
2 The title of her book
3 The amount of the accounting fraud

3 Guessing unknown words and phrases

Look at the words in bold in the text. With a partner, discuss their meanings.

4 Reading and predicting

Read the article about the renowned whistleblower, Cynthia Cooper, who exposed the problems of WorldCom. Look carefully at the sentences before and after the gaps and predict what kind of information is missing. Make notes for each gap.

WorldCom whistleblower Cynthia Cooper tells all

(1) _____ She became famous not by choice, but because of the WorldCom financial statement fraud valued at $11 billion. She was the Vice President of Internal Audit at WorldCom, a position that was not easily obtained. She almost **single-handedly** created the internal audit department at WorldCom, and her book *Extraordinary Circumstances: The Journey of a Corporate Whistleblower* details the struggle to get management to take internal audit seriously.

(2) _____ The company **went on an acquisition spree**, and the merging of many small companies, managers and accounting systems **was a disaster waiting to happen**. Cynthia says that WorldCom was much better at acquiring companies than integrating them, and that is clear.

(3) _____ There were too many small systems being pieced together, and it was easy for numbers and authorizations to get lost in the shuffle. This struggle is **well documented** by Cynthia, who no doubt **painstakingly** researched the various acquisitions in order to give such a complete history.

The process of uncovering the WorldCom fraud, as Cynthia and her team found out, was **gruelling**. Their investigation into the accounting **shenanigans** was long because the accounting entries behind this **manipulation** of the financial statements were complex. (4) _____ And the investigation was hard because management didn't want Cynthia and her people looking into the entries, for obvious reasons.

After the fraud became clear to Cynthia and her team, there was a long fight over whether something should or could be done about it. (5) _____ It is no surprise that there is no accounting rule that backs up what was done, because it wasn't done with the accounting rules in mind. It was done with only Wall Street in mind.

5 Matching missing sentences

Read the article again and choose the correct sentence (A–E) to fill each gap. There is one extra sentence which you will not need to use.

A Things started going wrong at WorldCom very early.

B Scott Sullivan was determined to find an accounting rule to justify the fraudulent accounting entries.

C Cynthia Cooper was a true corporate whistleblower.

D The story of the investigation comes to life through Cynthia's words.

E Hundreds of entries were made to a variety of accounts in order to confuse anyone who might later look at them.

F From an accounting perspective, it was next to impossible to create a properly controlled system

■ Section B Exam focus

1 Pre-reading

What do you know about the US bankruptcy procedures Chapters 7 and 11? Discuss with a partner.

2 Predicting missing words

Complete the descriptions of bankruptcy procedures in the USA with the words from the box. The first one (0) is given as an example. Discuss your choices with a partner.

> appointed   converts   ~~corporations~~   fiduciary   limits
> majority   property   possession   purposes   straight bankruptcy
> supervision   wiping out

Chapter 11 bankruptcy is a form of bankruptcy reorganization available to individuals, **(0)** _____corporations_____ and partnerships. It has no **(1)** _____ on the amount of debt, as Chapter 13 does. It is the usual choice for large businesses seeking to restructure their debt. The debtor usually remains in **(2)** _____ of its assets, and operates the business under the **(3)** _____ of the court and for the benefit of creditors. The debtor in possession is a **(4)** _____ for the creditors. If the management is ineffective or less than honest, a trustee may be **(5)** _____ . Individuals usually file Chapter 7 or Chapter 13 rather than Chapter 11.

Chapter 7 bankruptcy, sometimes called a **(6)** _____ , is a liquidation proceeding. The debtor turns over all non-exempt **(7)** _____ to the bankruptcy trustee, who then **(8)** _____ it to cash for distribution to the creditors. The debtor receives a discharge of all dischargeable debts, usually within four months. In the vast **(9)** _____ of cases, the debtor has no assets to lose, so Chapter 7 will give that person a relatively quick 'fresh start'. One of the main **(10)** _____ of bankruptcy law is to give a person who is hopelessly burdened with debt a fresh start by **(11)** _____ his or her debts. In a Chapter 7 case, however, a discharge is only available to individual debtors, not to partnerships or corporations.

EXAM TASK
Test of Reading Part 4

3 Multiple matching

Read the article on page 103 about the bankruptcy process in the USA. Choose the best sentence (A–H) to fill each of the gaps. There is one extra sentence which you do not need to use. The first one (0) is given as an example.

0 H

The bankruptcy process

Article I, Section 8, of the United States Constitution authorizes Congress to enact "uniform laws on the subject of bankruptcies." **(0)** _H_ The Bankruptcy Code, which is codified as title 11 of the United States Code, has been amended several times since its enactment. It is the uniform federal law that governs all bankruptcy cases.

The procedural aspects of the bankruptcy process are governed by the Federal Rules of Bankruptcy Procedure (often called the "Bankruptcy Rules") and local rules of each bankruptcy court. The Bankruptcy Rules contain a set of official forms for use in bankruptcy cases. **(1)** ____

There is a bankruptcy court for each judicial district in the country. Each state has one or more districts. There are 90 bankruptcy districts across the country. The bankruptcy courts generally have their own clerk's offices.

The court official with decision-making power over federal bankruptcy cases is the United States bankruptcy judge, a judicial officer of the United States district court. **(2)** ____ Much of the bankruptcy process is administrative, however, and is conducted away from the courthouse. In cases under Chapters 7, 12, or 13, and sometimes in Chapter 11 cases, this administrative process is carried out by a trustee who is appointed to oversee the case.

(3) ____ A typical Chapter 7 debtor will not appear in court and will not see the bankruptcy judge unless an objection is raised in the case. A Chapter 13 debtor may only have to appear before the bankruptcy judge at a plan confirmation hearing. Usually, the only formal proceeding at which a debtor must appear is the meeting of creditors, which is usually held at the offices of the U.S. trustee.

(4) ____ A fundamental goal of the federal bankruptcy laws enacted by Congress is to give debtors a financial "fresh start" from burdensome debts. The Supreme Court made this point about the purpose of the bankruptcy law in a 1934 decision: **(5)** ____

Local Loan Co. v. Hunt, 292 U.S. 234, 244 (1934). This goal is accomplished through the bankruptcy discharge, which releases debtors from personal liability from specific debts. **(6)** ____ This publication describes the bankruptcy discharge in a question-and-answer format, discussing the timing of the discharge, the scope of the discharge (what debts are discharged and what debts are not discharged), objections to discharge, and revocation of the discharge.

A The Bankruptcy Code and Bankruptcy Rules (and local rules) set forth the formal legal procedures for dealing with the debt problems of individuals and businesses.

B The bankruptcy judge may decide any matter connected with a bankruptcy case, such as eligibility to file or whether a debtor should receive a discharge of debts.

C A debtor's involvement with the bankruptcy judge is usually very limited.

D This meeting is informally called a "341 meeting" because section 341 of the Bankruptcy Code requires that the debtor attend this meeting so that creditors can question the debtor about debts and property.

E "It gives to the honest but unfortunate debtor … a new opportunity in life and a clear field for future effort, unhampered by the pressure and discouragement of preexisting debt."

F The cases are traditionally given the names of the chapters that describe them.

G At the same time, it prohibits creditors from ever taking any action against the debtor to collect those debts.

H Under this grant of authority, Congress enacted the "Bankruptcy Code" in 1978.

LISTENING

■ Section A **Skills**

1 Synonyms

Match the words on the left (1–8) with their synonyms on the right (a–h).

1	an allegation	**a**	legal action
2	proceedings	**b**	disgraced
3	wrongdoing	**c**	a penalty
4	a sanction	**d**	illegal activity
5	a proposition	**e**	distribution
6	discredited	**f**	a proposal
7	allocation	**g**	reputable
8	venerable	**h**	an accusation

2 🎧 60 10.1 Listening for detail

Listen to a presentation about recent corporate scandals and choose the correct answer (A, B or C) to these questions.

1 Nowadays, the business and financial world in the USA is more concerned than before about …
   A the flood of investigations regarding business fraud.
   B the credit crunch.
   C the number of bankruptcies in the financial sector.

2 The speaker mentions that several members of the management of corporations such as Enron have …
   A decided to leave the profession.
   B caused a serious crisis in America.
   C had to face legal action.

3 As a result of the investigations, Arthur Andersen has …
   A damaged the free-enterprise system.
   B been pushed out of the business.
   C faced bankruptcy.

4 The string of business scandals has …
   A had serious outcomes on US business and financial circles.
   B damaged the economy.
   C damaged the credibility of US corporates.

3 🎧 61 10.2 Listening and speaking

Listen to a court examiner talking about WorldCom and make notes. Then ask and answer these questions with a partner.

1 What was the speaker's role in the WorldCom case?

2 Where and when did WorldCom file for bankruptcy?

3 What was the problem with WorldCom's accounts?

4 Why is the WorldCom case of interest to the general public?

5 What is the speaker going to cover in his talk?

4 🎧 **62** **10.3 Listening and writing**

Listen to a bankruptcy examiner and complete these notes with not more than three words in each gap.

··

Role of a bankruptcy examiner

1 A bankruptcy examiner is appointed by the judge _____ court.

2 His/Her function is to perform _____ of the case.

3 Finally, he/she should _____ .

The WorldCom case

4 In the WorldCom case, the examiner had to identify _____ of action against the people responsible for losses.

5 The examiners co-operated with the US _____ , as well as the state prosecutors and regulators such as the SEC.

6 They also worked with representatives of the _____ to compile reports containing all the facts to assist the new management of WorldCom.

··

■ Section B **Exam focus**

1 Pre-listening

You are going to hear several speakers talking about the Insolvency Helpline. Before you listen, consider this question.

What services would you expect an Insolvency Helpline to offer, both for individuals and companies?

2 🎧 **63–67** **10.4–10.8 Identifying topics**

Listen to five speakers talking about the Insolvency Helpline. As you listen, write the number of each speaker next to the topic(s) he/she covers (A–K). One of the topics on the list is not mentioned by any of the speakers.

Topics   **Speaker**

A Benefits of using the Insolvency Helpline   ❏

B Financial assistance with divorce   ❏

C Current situation of consumer debt in the UK   ❏

D Problems with commercial debt-management companies   ❏

E TV advertising campaigns for commercial debt recovery   ❏

F Services provided by the Insolvency Helpline   ❏

G How to access the Helpline   ❏

H Description of the Insolvency Helpline   ❏

I The growth of commercial debt-management companies   ❏

J The aim of the Insolvency Helpline   ❏

K Self-help tools provided by the Helpline   ❏

SPEAKING

■ Section A Skills

1 Talking about insolvency

Work in pairs.

Student A: Read Fact Sheet A on page 114 and prepare a presentation for your partner covering these points:

● what an individual voluntary arrangement (IVA) is

● how an IVA is arranged

● what happens in an IVA

● some of the advantages of an IVA

Student B: Read Fact Sheet B on page 115 and prepare a presentation for your partner covering these points:

● what a company voluntary arrangement (CVA) is

● how a CVA is drawn up

● how a CVA works

● some of the advantages of a CVA

TRIVIA

Rembrandt, the famous Dutch painter, went bankrupt in 1656.

2 Bankruptcy forum

Consider these questions addressed to an online bankruptcy forum and answer them with a partner.

1 My company has been experiencing problems. and we currently face insolvency. What can we do in this situation? Are there any alternatives to bankruptcy?

2 I need some advice. Can anybody tell me more about bankruptcy? I mean, how do I petition for my bankruptcy? Is this advisable?

3 I was declared bankrupt by the court last year. How long does bankruptcy last, and how can I be discharged from bankruptcy?

4 Can you tell me what the main changes of the new legislation (Enterprise Act 2002) are, and will this enable me to make a fresh start?

5 How can my bankruptcy be reversed, and in what circumstances?

6 What is 'discharge from bankruptcy', and how can I obtain it?

7 For the past 18 months we have been having serious financial difficulties, and I am considering applying for bankruptcy. If I do so, what will happen to my business in bankruptcy? Will I be able to continue trading?

8 Is it cheaper to make myself bankrupt. What are the costs involved?

9 What happens if a Bankruptcy Restrictions Order (BRO) is placed on me, and what are the restrictions?

10 My company was declared bankrupt last month. What effect will bankruptcy have on my personal credit rating?

■ Section B **Exam focus**

Three-minute presentations

Using the skeleton notes, create interactive three-minute presentations for these three headlines.

UK SURGE OF BUSINESS FAILURES AS CREDIT CRUNCH HITS COMPANIES

- Experian report – UK corporate insolvency: up 8.5% this quarter
- problem business sectors – agriculture, banking, food retail and clothing
- 10% of failures – building and construction
- East Midlands worst – insolvencies up 53.6%
- creditors' voluntary liquidations up 14.1%
- compulsory liquidations down 2.2%, perhaps reinforcing concerns about confidence as most debtors choose CVLs, not compulsory winding-up
- growth of corporate rescue – administrations and company voluntary arrangements – 23.7% and 37.6% respectively

---

INCREASE IN IVAs STRENGTHEN DEBT-MANAGEMENT COMPANIES

- increase in media coverage of debt problems – TV, Internet, newspapers
- record level of bankruptcies in UK – easy access to credit
- debt-management companies – high growth, i.e. Debts.co.uk – 79% jump in turnover
- individual voluntary arrangements – very popular solution – allow individuals % payment of debt over a period
- banks are calling for tighter regulation – losing money – many customers opt for IVAs – result – lower recovery for banks

---

PWC PREDICT MORE INSOLVENCIES AHEAD

- accountancy firm PricewaterhouseCoopers predict increase in UK bankruptcies
- PWC predictions – higher mortgages – more people rely on credit cards – debts will increase
- backlog of individual voluntary arrangements (IVAs) – push up insolvency figures
- UK insolvency figures and credit-card debt down slightly, but PWC report 'precious plastic', predicts change in trend
- over-borrowing by consumers – leading to more personal insolvencies

---

▶ See **Language bank, Presentations**, page 118

WRITING

■ Section A **Skills**

1 Sequencing sentences in letters

Put these sentences in a letter from a debtor to a creditor in the correct order.

1 _H_ , 2 ____ , 3 ____ , 4 ____ , 5 ____ , 6 ____ , 7 ____ , 8 ____ , 9 ____ , 10 ____

A I also request that, if accepted, you will mark any entry on a credit-reference agency file relating to the above account as 'satisfied in full'.

B Yours faithfully

C However, I can raise £2,800 and I want to offer this as an ex-gratia payment in full and final settlement of the account.

D I look forward to receiving your reply.

E This offer is made on the clear understanding that, if accepted, neither you or any associate company will take any other action to enforce or pursue this debt in any way whatsoever and that I will be released from any liability.

F Payment can be made within ten days of receiving your written agreement of this offer and method of payment.

G Re: Account No/Reference No: 66-55-101 Arrears £ 4,032

H Dear Sir/Madam

I I can confirm that I am unable to pay the money which I owe in full as I am currently unable to work due to illness.

J I write with reference to the money which you are claiming on the above account.

2 Word forms

Complete these sentences with words formed from the base words in brackets.

1 The Financial Director faces _____ of fraud for modifying the company's financial statements. (ALLEGE)

2 Many people believe that there is a crisis in corporate _____ nowadays. (GOVERN)

3 Members of the top management of leading corporations have been involved in legal _____ . (PROCEED)

4 Cynthia Cooper found several _____ in the accounts of WorldCom. (ILLEGAL)

5 In recent years, many corporations such as Tyco and Adelphia have been plagued by _____ activities. (FRAUD)

6 At Enron, massive accounting _____ were discovered by auditors. (REGULAR)

7 My _____ as bankruptcy examiner in the WorldCom case came after 25 years in the forensic accounting business. (APPOINT)

8 The court reports will are available to the public for their _____ in similar cases. (GUIDE)

9 Unfortunately, there are many examples of the _____ of corporate governance in the USA. (FAIL)

10 My _____ to clients is always to look at ways of avoiding bankruptcy. (RECOMMEND)

■ Section B **Exam focus**

EXAM TASK
Test of Writing Part 1

1 Writing a letter

You work for a firm of accountants. One of your clients, Marcus Kitchens, has had initial meetings with CVP, a company that provides venture capital, and hopes to raise funds build new warehouse facilities. You have recently received a letter from CVP regarding your client's application for funds.

Read this letter from Ross Aziz, Director of Venture Capital Operations at CVP, in which he queries certain aspects of your client's application. Then, using all the information in the notes, write a reply (120–180 words) on behalf of your client.

I am writing regarding your client, Marcus Kitchens, which has recently put in an application for venture capital to build a new warehouse.

Firstly, we noted from the accounts that the company has shown significant growth during the last year. Could you explain the reasons for such a high level of growth? ◄———

> reasons – unique, high-quality products

We also note from the application that the estimates for construction of the new warehouse were 20% higher than the original figure we discussed with Hugh Marcus. Can you explain why? ◄———

> architect submitted plans for larger facility – with show kitchens

Thirdly, we note that the accounts show a 50% increase in contractors' fees in the last year. Could you clarify this situation? ◄———

> Marcus Kitchens expanded services to provide installation as well as kitchens

Finally, we understand that the DIY market, especially kitchens, is highly competitive and wonder if the projected sales figures and the projections for market share are realistic. ◄———

> exclusive suppliers to hotel chains – company has carried out in-depth market study

We look forward to your reply.

Yours sincerely,

Ross Aziz
Director
Calculus Venture Partners

EXAM TASK
Test of Writing Part 2

2 Writing a report

One of your clients is having financial difficulties and is considering entering into a company voluntary arrangement (CVA) as opposed to administration or liquidation. Prior to a meeting with the directors of the firm, she has asked you to compile a brief report. Write the report (200–250 words), explaining the following points. If necessary, refer to Fact Sheet B on page 115.

- what a CVA is a what it involves
- how a CVA proposal is made
- the approval process
- the advantages of entering into a CVA
- how your firm can help with the CVA process

TIP
In the Test of Writing, make sure that you have time at the end to check your work and correct any errors you may have made.

▶ See **Language bank, Linking ideas**, page 119

Mini-presentation 1: GAAP

GAAP are the common set of accounting principles, standards and procedures that companies use to compile their financial statements in the USA. They are a combination of authoritative standards (set by policy boards) and simply the commonly accepted ways of recording and reporting accounting information. GAAP are imposed on companies so that investors have a minimum level of consistency in the financial statements they use when analyzing companies for investment purposes. GAAP cover such things as revenue recognition, balance-sheet item classification and outstanding share measurements. Companies are expected to follow GAAP rules when reporting their financial data via financial statements. If a financial statement is not prepared using GAAP principles, be very wary!

That said, keep in mind that GAAP is only a set of standards. There is plenty of room within GAAP for unscrupulous accountants to distort figures. So, even when a company uses GAAP, you still need to scrutinize its financial statements.

Mini-presentation 2: CMA

The title 'Certified Management Accountant' is a professional designation awarded by various professional bodies around the world. The CMA designation is a post-nominal award issued to individuals who have achieved a peer-based criteria of professional competency in the field of management accounting. Management accounting qualifications differ from those such as the ACA or CPA 'Chartered' or 'Public' accounting qualifications in a number of ways, but primarily management accountants are focused on internal cost measures and accounting for management review, whereas ACA/CPA specialists are focused on the reporting of financial results to external bodies such as tax departments, capital markets, investors and others.

The CMA qualification is offered in Australia, Canada, the United States and many other developed countries. CMA is a granted certificate from a professional body like the Institute of Certified Management Accountants (ICMA) or the Institute of Management Accountants (IMA), provided that the candidate passed a rigorous examination and met educational and practical experience requirements. Due to the non-statutory status in United States, a CMA generally provides their services directly to their employers rather than to the public. A CMA may also provide services to the public, but to a much lesser extent than a Certified Public Accountant (CPA).

The CMA credentials differ significantly from the CPA designation. More than 80% of accounting professionals in the USA work within organizations, building quality financial practices into the organization through decision support, planning and control over the organization's value-creating operations. For these managerial finance and accounting professionals, the CMA may be more appropriate as a best selection. Many professional accountants hold both CPA and CMA designations.

Mini-presentation 3: ACCA

ACCA (the Association of Chartered Certified Accountants) is the largest and fastest-growing global professional accountancy body, with 296,000 students and 115,000 members in 170 countries. We aim to offer the first-choice qualifications to people of application, ability and ambition around the world who seek a rewarding career in accountancy, finance and management. We support our students and members throughout their careers, providing services through a network of nearly 80 offices and centres. We have established more than 50 global accountancy partnerships, through which we deliver qualifications and a range of services which promote global standards, benefit the accountancy profession and enhance the value of accountants in the workplace. We work closely with more than 470 registered tuition providers and nearly 8,500 employers of accountants and finance professionals. We use our expertise and experience to work with governments, donor agencies and professional bodies to develop the accountancy profession. We aim to achieve and promote the highest professional, ethical and governance standards and advance the public interest. ACCA's reputation is grounded in over 100 years of providing accounting and finance qualifications. Our long traditions are complemented by modern thinking, backed by a diverse, global membership.

Mini-presentation 4: CIMA

CIMA – the Chartered Institute of Management Accountants – is a leading membership body that offers an internationally recognized professional qualification in management accountancy, which focuses on accounting for business.

As an organization, we are committed to constant improvement, and our reputation as a professional and regulatory body has never been stronger. We are increasingly the first choice for students and employers.

CIMA upholds high ethical and professional standards to maintain public confidence in management accountancy. Our members and students must adhere to CIMA's ethical guidelines, byelaws and regulations. All CIMA's governance activities – overseen by the Council and its committees – underpin the commitment to maintain the professional standards and competence of our members and students.

CIMA is the voice of over 164,000 members and students in 161 countries. It is responsible for the education and training of management accountants who work in industry, commerce, not-for-profit and public sector organizations.

Qualifying Management Accountants

CIMA works with some of the world's leading employers and course providers around the world to educate, train and qualify first-class financial managers. We pride ourselves on the commercial relevance of our syllabus, which is regularly updated to reflect the latest business developments and employer needs. This means CIMA graduates are in demand by all forward-looking businesses. As well as the CIMA Professional Qualification, we offer the CIMA Certificate in Business Accounting and the CIMA Advanced Diploma in Management Accounting.

Supporting our members

We offer valuable guidance, support, information and training to our members at every stage of their careers. And because CIMA members are in touch with the latest industry developments, they are ideally qualified to lead the finance function in any organization.

Upholding high professional standards

It has never been more important for accountants to demonstrate total integrity. CIMA plays an essential role in protecting the public interest by regulating its members and contributing to the ongoing development of the profession through technical research and development.

Mini-presentation 5: AICPA

The fundamental purpose of the AICPA

The American Institute of Certified Public Accountants (AICPA) is the national, professional organization for all Certified Public Accountants. Its mission is to provide members with the resources, information and leadership that enable them to provide valuable services in the highest professional manner to benefit the public, as well as employers and clients. In fulfilling its mission, the AICPA works with state CPA organizations and gives priority to those areas where public reliance on CPA skills is most significant.

AICPA objectives

(The major areas of activity to pursue in carrying out the Institute's mission.)
To achieve its mission, the Institute:

A Advocacy

Serves as the national representative of CPAs before governments, regulatory bodies and other organizations in protecting and promoting members' interests.

B Certification and licensing

Seeks the highest possible level of uniform certification and licensing standards and promotes and protects the CPA designation.

C Communications

Promotes public awareness and confidence in the integrity, objectivity, competence and professionalism of CPAs and monitors the needs and views of CPAs.

D Recruiting and education

Encourages highly qualified individuals to become CPAs and supports the development of outstanding academic programmes.

E Standards and performance

Establishes professional standards; assists members in continually improving their professional conduct, performance and expertise; and monitors such performance to enforce current standards and requirements.

Mini-presentation 6: FSA

The Chancellor of the Exchequer announced the reform of financial services regulation in the UK and the creation of a new regulator on 20 May 1997.

The Chancellor announced his decision to merge banking supervision and investment services regulation into the Securities and Investments Board (SIB). The SIB formally changed its name to the Financial Services Authority (FSA) in October 1997.

The first stage of the reform of financial services regulation was completed in June 1998, when responsibility for banking supervision was transferred to the FSA from the Bank of England. In May 2000, the FSA took over the role of UK Listing Authority from the London Stock Exchange. The Financial Services and Markets Act, which received Royal Assent in June 2000 and was implemented on 1 December 2001, transferred to the FSA the responsibilities of several other organizations.

The FSA is an independent non-governmental body, given statutory powers by the Financial Services and Markets Act 2000. It is a company limited by guarantee and financed by the financial services industry. The Treasury appoints the FSA Board, which currently consists of a chairman, a chief executive officer, three managing directors, and nine non-executive directors (including a lead non-executive member, the deputy chairman). This Board sets our overall policy, but day-to-day decisions and management of the staff are the responsibility of the executive.

It is an independent body that regulates the financial services industry in the UK.

It has been given a wide range of rule-making, investigatory and enforcement powers in order to meet its four statutory objectives. In meeting these, it is also obliged to have regard to the Principles of Good Regulation.

Mini-presentation 7: EAA

The European Accounting Association (EAA) aims to link together the Europe-wide community of accounting scholars and researchers, to provide a platform for the wider dissemination of European accounting research, and to foster and improve research.

Since its establishment in 1977, the EAA has had a major impact on the accounting research community throughout Europe. Gone are the days when only a few accounting academics knew their colleagues in other countries. The EAA has established a secure and developing series of networks that bring together all accounting researchers interested in a wider European concept of their subject and research interests.

Mini-presentation 8: IFAC

The International Federation of Accountants (IFAC) was founded on 7 October 1977 in Munich, Germany, at the 11th World Congress of Accountants. The organization's headquarters have been based in New York City since its founding.

IFAC was established to strengthen the worldwide accountancy profession in the public interest by:

● developing high-quality international standards and supporting their adoption and use;
● facilitating collaboration and co-operation among its member bodies;
● collaborating and co-operating with other international organizations; and
● serving as the international spokesperson for the accountancy profession.

Mini-presentation 9: CITP

A Certified Information Technology Professional (CITP) is a Certified Public Accountant recognized for their technology expertise and unique ability to bridge the gap between business and technology. Unlike other certifications that recognize only a narrow scope of skills, the CITP credential recognizes technical expertise across a wide range of business-technology practice areas.

The CITP credential is predicated on the fact that in today's complex business environment, technology plays an ever-increasing role in how organizations meet their business obligations, and that no single professional has a more comprehensive understanding of those obligations than a Certified Public Accountant. An increasingly competitive global marketplace has organizations clamouring for new technologies and the capacities, efficiencies and advantages they afford. While IT professionals have the technical expertise necessary to ensure that technology solutions are properly deployed, they lack the CPA's perspective and ability to understand the complicated business implications associated with technology. The CITP credential encourages and recognizes excellence in the delivery of technology-related services by CPA professionals, and provides tools, training and support to help CPAs expand their IT-related services and provide greater benefit to the business and academic communities they serve.

Mini-presentation 10: CIPFA

The Chartered Institute of Public Finance and Accountancy (CIPFA) is one of the leading professional accountancy bodies in the UK and the only one which specializes in the public sector. It is responsible for the education and training of professional accountants and for their regulation through the setting and monitoring of professional standards. Uniquely among the professional accountancy bodies in the UK, CIPFA has responsibility for setting accounting standards for a significant part of the economy, namely local government.

CIPFA's members work, often at the most senior levels, in public-service bodies, in the national audit agencies and major accountancy firms. They are respected throughout for their high technical and ethical standards, and professional integrity. CIPFA also provides a range of high-quality advisory, information and training and consultancy services to public-service organizations. Our weekly magazine, *Public Finance*, is widely read by elected representatives and officials in all tiers and corners of government. As such, CIPFA can justifiably lay claim to be the leading independent commentator on managing and accounting for public money.

Mini-presentation 11: GAAS

Generally Accepted Auditing Standards (GAAS) are a set of systematic guidelines used by auditors when conducting audits on companies' finances, ensuring the accuracy, consistency and verifiability of auditors' actions and reports. By relying on GAAS, auditors can minimize the probability of missing material information. GAAS are divided into these main sections:

1 general standards.
2 standards of fieldwork.
3 standards of reporting.

Each section is littered with requirements that the auditor and the subject company must meet. In short, an auditor must adequately plan the audit in advance, be independent of the client at all times, and always obtain reliable evidence. The companies must present their financial statements in accordance with GAAS, remain consistent in their reporting, and explicitly disclose all pertinent information.

Mini-presentation 12: AQF

Audit Quality Forum (AQF) calls for audits to be more open. The audit report is a signed document expressing the truth and fairness of a company's financial statements, which goes to the heart of discussions around transparency and confidence in the independent audit. The AQF working group on auditor reporting was tasked with considering whether the wording of the audit report satisfies shareholders' expectations. To achieve this, the group considered the information that shareholders wish to see within the audit report, why they require this information and whether the current audit report meets their needs.

The paper recommends that the audit report should, within a clearly defined framework and in line with applicable European Commission (EC) requirements, include the following:

● an opinion paragraph adopting as soon as practicable the wording and structure of Section 495(3) of the Companies Act 2006 in its three distinct parts. Clearly, the wording of audit reports will have to comply with the law from the effective date of the Companies Act 2006 regardless of whether there is early adoption;

● a positive statement that adequate accounting records have been kept;

● a positive statement that there are no matters that auditors wish to draw attention to by way of emphasis under Section 235(2A)(b) of the Companies Act 1985 or Section 495(4)(b) of the Companies Act 2006;

● improvements in the readability of audit reports by moving the opinion to the front and much of the standardized boilerplate text to the back or into an appendix

Unit 10, Speaking, Skills, Exercise 1

FACT SHEET A: INDIVIDUAL VOLUNTARY ARRANGEMENT

What is an IVA?

An individual voluntary arrangement (IVA) is a formal agreement between an individual and his/her creditors. The individual makes an arrangement with his/her creditors to make reduced payments towards the total amount of his/her debt in order to pay off a percentage of what he/she owes. Generally, after five years, the debt is classed as settled.

How does an IVA work?

Due to its formal nature, an IVA has to be set up by a licensed professional (an insolvency practitioner). Firstly, the individual is asked questions regarding his/her current financial situation. Based on this information, a repayment amount is agreed. Then the proposal for the IVA is drawn up by an insolvency practitioner. An application may then be made to the court for an Interim Order. Once this is in place, no creditors will be able to take legal action against the individual. A creditor meeting will be arranged, which the individual should attend. If the creditors agree to the IVA, it is approved.

The IVA is legally binding. As long the repayments are made, when the term of the agreement is finished, the individual will be free of the debts, regardless of how much has been paid off. During the period of the arrangement, the financial situation of the individual is regularly reviewed to see if there has been any change in his/her circumstances.

Some advantages of an IVA

1 **Privacy**

   An IVA is a private agreement with creditors. This means that no one else needs to be told about it, so there is no negative publicity.

2 **No professional disqualification**

   If an IVA is set up, the professional or employment status of the individual will not be affected; he/she can carry on running his/her own business and acting as a director. If someone is made bankrupt, he/she is not allowed to be involved in promoting, forming or managing a company without the permission of the court.

3 **Costs**

   Setting up an IVA is less costly for the debtor and creditor than a bankruptcy procedure.

4 **No loss of assets**

   With an IVA, the individual can keep his/her assets. If someone is made bankrupt, then all his/her assets are vested in the trustee, and they might have to be sold to repay the debts.

Other benefits of IVAs

- Up to 75% of the debt can be written off with an IVA.
- With an IVA, monthly repayments are based on what the individual can afford.
- When the IVA is completed according to the specified terms, the individual is considered to be debt-free.

Unit 10, Speaking, Skills, Exercise 1

FACT SHEET B: COMPANY VOLUNTARY ARRANGEMENT

What is a CVA?

A company voluntary arrangement (CVA) is an insolvency procedure that allows a financially troubled company to reach a binding agreement with its creditors about payment of all, or part, of its debts over an agreed period of time.

How is a CVA drawn up?

A CVA proposal is drafted by the directors with the assistance of a licensed insolvency practitioner, known as the 'nominee'. The proposals are then sent to the court, the creditors and the shareholders, giving them 14 days' notice of the CVA creditors' meeting.

How does a CVA work?

The nominee (an insolvency practitioner) reports to the court to arrange a meeting of creditors and shareholders to consider the proposal. The meeting decides whether to approve the CVA. If the meeting of creditors and shareholders approves a CVA, the nominee becomes the supervisor of the CVA. When the CVA has been carried out, the company's liability to its creditors is cleared.

Some advantages of a CVA

1 **No interruption to business**

   The company can continue trading during the CVA and afterwards.

2 **Cost effective**

   It provides a cost-effective way of avoiding outright insolvency for a company with financial problems.

3 **Saves face**

   There is no stigma to a CVA compared to going into liquidation, so the reputation of the business is not affected.

4 **Gives the company time**

   It assists businesses that have experienced trading difficulties since start up and need time to prove their business model.

5 **Helps with short-term problems**

   It helps businesses which will be profitable in the long term, but which are under pressure from creditors.

6 **Helps restructuring**

   It helps businesses that need some time to put together a new business plan or restructure the company.

7 **No investigation**

   A CVA avoids the need for the licensed insolvency practitioner to investigate the affairs of the company.

Useful abbreviations

ABFA	American Board of Forensic Accounting
ABV	Accredited Business Valuation (*specialist*)
ACCA	Association of Chartered Certified Accountants
ACV	actual cash value
AICPA	American Institute of Certified Public Accountants
APB	Auditing Practices Board
APV	adjusted present value
ARR	accounting rate of return
ASB	Accounting Standards Board
ATF	Accounting Task Force
BAS	Board for Accounting Standards
BRIC	Brazil, Russia, India and China (*world affairs*)
BSC	balanced score card
CA	Chartered Accountant
CAT	Certified Accounting Technician
CBA	computer-based assessment
CCA	current cost accounting
CCAB	Consultative Committee of Accountancy Bodies
CFO	Chief Financial Officer
CGT	capital gains tax
CIB	Chartered Institute of Bankers
CICA	Canadian Institute of Chartered Accountants
CIMA	Chartered Institute of Management Accountants
CIPFA	Chartered Institute of Public Finance and Accountancy
CPA	Certified Public Accountant
CPE	continuing professional education
CPI	consumer price index
CPP	current purchasing power
CSR	corporate social responsibility
CV	curriculum vitae
CVA	Certified Valuation Analyst
CVA	company voluntary agreement/arrangement
CVL	company voluntary liquidation
CVP	cost–volume–profit (*analysis*)
e&oe	errors and omissions excepted
EBITDA	earnings before interest, tax, depreciation and amortization
EFRAG	European Financial Reporting Advisory Group
EMS	European monetary system
EPS	earnings per share
EVA	economic value added
FASB	Financial Accounting Standards Board
FCCA	Fellow Member of the Association of Chartered Certified Accountants
FCF	financial cashflow
FDI	foreign direct investment
FIFO	first in, first out
FRC	Financial Reporting Council

FRRP	Financial Reporting Review Panel
FSF	Financial Stability Forum
FTVA	fast-track voluntary arrangement
GAAP	generally accepted accounting principles
GAAS	generally accepted auditing standards
IAD	Insurance Accounts Directive
IAS	International Accounting Standards
IASB	International Accounting Standards Board
IASC	International Accounting Standards Committee
IASCF	International Accounting Standards Committee Foundation
ICAEW	Institute of Chartered Accountants in England and Wales
ICAS	Institute of Chartered Accountants of Scotland
ICF	investing cash flow
ID	identity
IFRS	International Financial Reporting Standards
IPO	initial public offering
IPT	insurance premium tax
IRR	internal rate of return
IRS	Inland Revenue Service
IVA	individual voluntary arrangement
LLP	limited liability partnership
LTV	lifetime value
MMC	Monopolies and Mergers Commission
MVA	market value added
NPV	net present value
OBS	off balance sheet (*banking*)
OFT	Office of Fair Trading
OECD	Organisation for Economic Co-operation and Development
P/E	price/earnings (*ratio*)
PCAOB	Public Company Accounting Oversight Board
POB	Professional Oversight Board
PRDB	purchases returns day book
PwC	PricewaterhouseCoopers
REIT	Real Estate Investment Trust
ROE	return on equity
ROI	return on investment
RPM	resale price maintenance
SAS	Statement of Auditing Standard
SEC	Securities Commission
SFC	Securities and Futures Commission
SME	small and medum-sized enterprise
SORP	statement of recommended practice
SOX	Sarbanes-Oxley Act of 2002
SQC	smaller quoted companies
SSAP	Statement of Standard Accountancy Practice (UK)
SWOT	strengths, weaknesses, opportunities and threats
TC	Test of Competence
VAT	value-added tax
WACC	weighted average cost of capital

Language bank

Presentations

Welcoming the audience
It gives me great pleasure to welcome you here this morning.
I'd like to welcome you on behalf of (the board of directors).

Introducing and welcoming speakers
I think you all know (Mrs Tahal), our (Marketing Director).
I'd like to introduce (Mr Peters), who represents (Hall & Partners).

Opening the presentation
The purpose of this presentation is to present / outline / explain …
I'd like to give you some information about …
My presentation today is about …
Today I'm going to talk about …
This morning, I'll begin by explaining …
I would like to begin by giving a brief overview of the situation.
Today, I'd like to tell you something about the company's performance last year.

Outlining the main points
There are four main areas to be considered …
My presentation today covers (three) main points.

Sequencing
I'll begin by looking at …
Then I'll explain …
Firstly / Secondly / Thirdly …
First / Then / After that / Finally …

Explain why something is interesting / significant
The information presented here today is important, as it shows …
If we compare this year's figures with last year's, it is interesting to note that …

Establishing a bridge
So, first of all, I'd like to …
Let's now move on to look at …
This brings me to my next point.
My next point is …
I'd now like to turn to …

Linking with a previous point
As I mentioned earlier, …
As I said at the beginning / in my introduction, …
To go back to …

Summarizing the main topics
To sum up, I'd like to say that …
So, to conclude …
In conclusion, we can see that …
To summarize, I feel that …

Making a strong final comment
It is clear from the figures presented here today that …
Given the data / information I have presented, we can be certain that …

Thanking your audience
I appreciate your being here today and thank you for your attention.
It has been a pleasure to be able to speak before you today, and I thank you for your attendance.
Finally, I'd like to thank you for coming today.
Thank you for your attention.

Discussions

Introducing a topic
Today, I am going to talk about …
First of all, I'd like to say / point out that …

Moving on to another point
Moving on, …
Let's move on to the second point.
The second point I want to make is …

Inviting participation
Would you like to add something to that?
Would you like to comment on that?

Giving examples
For example, …
To be more specific, …
For instance, …
Let me give you an example.

Clarifying comments
In other words, …
Let me put it another way.
The point I want to make is …

Asking for clarification
If I understood you correctly, you mean …
I'm not sure I follow you. Could you explain that again, please?
Could you elaborate on this point?
Could you clarify your last point?

Interrupting
Let me interrupt for a minute.
Could I just come in at this point?
Can I add something here?

Redirecting the discussion
That's not really relevant.
Let's keep to the point.

Highlighting points
Let me emphasize at this point, that …
I'd like to stress that …
This underlines the fact that …

Summarizing and concluding
To summarize …
In summary …
To conclude …
In conclusion …
The conclusions we can draw from this are …
To sum up, …
Right, let's sum up, shall we?
I'd like now to recap …
Let's summarize briefly what we've looked at.
Finally, let me remind you of some of the points we've covered.
If I can just sum up the main points …

Giving opinions

Asking for opinions/reactions
What do you think, (John)?
How do you feel about that, (Hana)?
I'd like to hear your view on this matter.
What's your reaction to that?
Where exactly do you stand on this issue?

Giving strong opinions
I firmly believe that we should (introduce more ATMs).
I'm absolutely convinced that we should (go ahead).
There's no doubt in my mind that this would be the best solution.

Giving neutral opinions
In my opinion, we should (install Sage).
Personally, I think we should (expand our headquarters).
I think we should (employ more administrative staff).
As I see it, (the firm needs stricter financial procedures).

Giving tentative opinions
It seems to me that we should (increase our range of services).
I tend to think we should (reduce our overheads).

Strong agreement
I completely agree.
I'm in total agreement.
Absolutely.

Neutral agreement
I agree.
I think you're right.

Partial agreement
I would tend to agree.
I agree in principle, but …
I agree to some extent, but …
By and large, I agree.
I see your point, but …

Strong disagreement
(I'm afraid) I totally disagree with you / I disagree entirely.
(I'm sorry,) I think you are mistaken.

Presenting arguments

Introducing your viewpoint
The first thing we have to consider …
The first thing to be considered …
One of the main arguments against / in favour of x is that …
There is no doubt that …
It is a fact that …
In my opinion, / Personally, / As far as I'm concerned, …

Agreement/disagreement
I agree/disagree with x when he/she writes/says that …

Partial disagreement
… but/however, …
… on the other hand, …

Definite agreement
I completely/totally agree with x.

Neutral agreement
X may be correct/true
a relevant point

Linking ideas

Writing in lists
firstly; secondly; thirdly; to begin with
next; then; after that; finally; lastly

Giving examples
for example; for instance; namely
in particular; particularly; especially; mainly; chiefly
In other words, … ; That is to say, …
as in the following examples; as follows; such as

Expressing alternatives
On the one hand, … , on the other hand, …
alternatively; rather; one alternative is …
Another possibility is … ; Another way of looking at this is …
by contrast; in comparison; on the contrary

Expressing the same idea in a different way
To put it simply, …
In other words, … ; In this case, …
In view of this, …
Looking at this another way, …

Adding more information
besides; also; moreover; furthermore; in addition
further; what is more; above all; as well as
either; neither … nor; not only … but also
in the same way; similarly; indeed
regarding; as for; with respect to
in reality; in theory; in fact

Emphasizing/contrasting a point already made
however; nonetheless; although; though
despite … ; in spite of … ; … nothwithstanding, …
While x may be true, …

Giving results
The result is …; The consequence is …
so; hence; thus; resulting from
accordingly; therefore; because of this
due to …

Summarizing and concluding
To sum up, …; To summarize, …; In short, …; On the whole, …
in brief; briefly; overall; thus
My conclusion is, …; To conclude, …

Handling questions

Giving a positive response
That's a good / a tricky / a difficult / an interesting question.
Thank you for asking that question. I can say that …
I'm glad someone asked that question.

Clarifying a question
If I understand you correctly, you want to know …
You're asking me about … . Is that right?
Sorry, I didn't follow / catch the question.
Could you repeat that for me, please?
Could you clarify what you mean?
In other words, you're asking …

Referring back
As I mentioned in the introduction, …
As I said in the first part of my presentation, …
As I said/explained at the beginning / earlier, …
I think I already mentioned that …

Checking your answer
Does that answer your question?
Is that clear?
Can we move on?

Accepting criticism
I agree up to a point.
I accept that.
That's a fair comment.
I agree with what you're saying.

Avoiding questions
Let me ask you the same question.
Let me ask you what you think.
I can answer that by asking you a question.
I'm afraid I can't really answer that.
I'm not in a position to answer that.
That's not really my area / field, I'm afraid.

Wrong topic
That's not really my field.
I'm afraid that question isn't really relevant to today's presentation.
I'm afraid that's confidential.
I'm not in a position to give you that information.
I'd be happy to discuss that with you in person after the presentation.

Hedging
Well, that depends on what you mean by …
There are, of course, several ways of looking at it.

Describing the activities of your firm/department

Starting
I'd now like to tell you about …
It consists of …
It is divided into …… sections / areas / branches.

Describing functions
Firstly, let's take a look at …
This department / section is responsible for …
                    is involved in …
                    is concerned with …
                    cooperates with …
                    deals with …
                    liaises with …

Moving on
Let's move on to …

Ending
Finally, I'd like to say a few words about …

Clarifying and explaining

Asking for clarification
What exactly do you mean by …?
Could you explain what you mean by …?
Could you clarify that?
Could you be more specific?
Could you give me an example?

Explaining
What I mean is …
What I am saying is …
… is another way of saying that …

Structuring a composition

Introducing opinions
In my opinion, …
Some people believe …
Most people tend to think that …

Contrasting
On the other hand, …
However, …

Giving examples
In most cases, …
Generally, …
In some cases, …
The main advantage …
In addition, …

Summarizing
In conclusion, …
To sum up, …

Expressing yourself emphatically

We categorically deny [doing] …
In no way did I [do] …
We fully recognize [that] …
I am completely aware of [the situation].
We enthusiastically endorse …
I happily, and completely believe [that] …
We freely appreciate [that] …
I certainly understand [that] …
We positively encourage [someone] to [do something].
We deeply regret [doing] …
I am very sorry about [doing] …
We readily endorse …
I strongly recommend [that] …
I really think you should [do] …
We totally reject …
I refuse to believe [that] …
We sincerely hope [that] …
I honestly think [that] …

Audio transcripts

1 Introduction to ICFE

1.1

OK … OK, everybody. Um, before I begin my presentation today, I'd like to take you back to a time many years ago and say a few words about a man who is responsible for the real start of accounting. He has often been called 'the father of accounting'. As you all know, during the Italian Renaissance, Venice operated as the business centre of Europe. Not surprisingly, it was here among merchants and traders that accounting was invented and practised. In 1445, Luca Pacioli, who went on to become a mathematician, was born in Sansepolcro, Tuscany. Years later, in 1494, Pacioli, who was known to be a friend of Leonardo da Vinci, went on to publish the influential book *Summa*, a summary of all the mathematics known at that time.

In fact, we owe much to Pacioli. Apart from the concept of double-entry accounting, Pacioli's ledger included assets-receivables and inventories-liabilities, capital, income, and expense accounts. He described the year-end closing entries and proposed that a trial balance should be used to prove a balanced ledger. In addition, his *Summa* made reference to the certification of books, ethics and cost accounting.

1.2

Speaker 1

This book was recommended to me by a colleague. In my view, it's essential for all students sitting accountancy exams on international financial reporting standards. Um, what's unique is that each chapter starts with a background of the issues giving rise to the standard, which I'm convinced is a much better approach than starting with aims and objectives.

1.3

Speaker 2

I've got a terrible memory when it comes to learning rules and procedures, so I was looking for something with a clear visual layout. When I picked up this book in the bookshop, I couldn't believe how clear it was. The text is teeming with colour illustrations of memory devices and diagrams to assist you in remembering the key points.

1.4

Speaker 3

I was studying accounting standards and just couldn't comprehend them, so I was desperately trying to find a suitable book, something simple but precise. The best thing about this book is its jargon-free presentation, which makes it easy to follow, so if you ask me, it's a must for anyone who wants to get to grips with the language of accounting standards.

1.5

Speaker 4

I was preparing a seminar and was looking for something easy to read which would also provide a good base for discussion. If you want a clear breakdown of accounting standards, er, the book includes full-colour key cards, which I cut out and use for revision purposes. So, whether you're starting out with the orange pages or a more advanced student (er, green pages), interested in group accounts (blue) or looking for something seriously advanced (red), you can locate information easily.

1.6

Speaker 5

I was looking for a basic overview of the individual standards – but nothing too theoretical – for a presentation I was asked to give at work. The best thing about the book is that it's written in surprisingly plain English, so basically it's like a key to solving accounting standards.

2 The financial environment

2.1

Good morning, everyone. The purpose of my presentation is to tell you what makes ICAS stand out from other professional bodies of accountants. Let's start with a brief overview of ICAS in figures. First of all, ICAS was the first professional body of accountants in the world, founded in 1854. It was also the first and only institute in the UK allowed to use the 'CA' designation.

Let's move on to the slides: 56% of ICAS members work in industry or commerce. Next, 66% of students are based in England and 34% in Scotland, and 94% of graduates recruited possess a first- or upper-second-class honours degree. Now, let's see … students and members of ICAS. There is a total of 2,400 students UK-wide and 16,000 members worldwide. Moving on to its growth rate, a 94% growth rate makes ICAS the fastest-growing accountancy body in the UK.

2.2

A: Can you give me some information about training to become a CA?

B: Yes, of course. What did you want to know?

A: I wanted to find out about how I can apply for a training contract.

B: Well, to train to become a CA, you must secure a training contract with an organization authorized by ICAS. This can be either a firm of chartered accountants or an industrial, commercial or public services organization. Currently, there are over 1,000 training vacancies throughout the UK, with a wide range of employers.

A: So, as a graduate, what do I need to apply for a CA training contract?

B: You need a UK degree or the overseas equivalent in any subject. Although some employers only accept applications from graduates with an ICAS-accredited accountancy degree, most accept those with any degree subject. Each employer has its own additional minimum entry requirements. Most employers are looking for strong academic performance, both at school and university. In some cases, there may be exemptions from some of the exams.

A: Really? Can you explain how that works?

B: Well, depending on the relevance of your degree subject, you can be exempt from some of the five exams at Test of Competence. Those with ICAS-accredited accountancy degrees may be eligible for up to five exemptions from TC. Er, you really need to speak to someone in the CA Education department to find out what exemptions you may be eligible for.

2.3

Adviser: Let's look at covering letters, and how they complement your CV and job application. What are your views on this, Tony?

Tony: If you ask me, I think that covering letters are often overlooked when applicants are applying for accountancy positions. I think this is a big mistake. In fact, it doesn't matter if you're applying for a job or writing a speculative letter to a company, your covering letter could make the difference between getting a foot in the door to a new job or having the door slammed in your face. Um, how do you feel about this, Chanelle?

Chanelle: I agree. Remember, covering letters are not just sent as a courtesy, but they are actually an introduction to a potential employer, aren't they, Aydin?

Aydin: Exactly. Covering letters should be designed to complement your CV and provide extra information about you. The covering letter is the first impression a potential employer will have of you, and without a good impact, they may not progress far with your CV, don't you think, Hans?

Hans: Er, I'm not convinced that's true. I think in large accounting firms, often the person who decides whether or not to interview you doesn't have time to look at everyone's covering letter. Er, what's your view on that, Sophie?

Sophie: I'm not sure about that. Anyway, in my view, I wouldn't want to work for a firm that can't be bothered to read a short covering letter.

2.4

Ad: OK. I think we've established that the covering letter is a key part of your written application, so let's consider the contents of the letter and the key points it should contain. What do you think, Chanelle?

C: Well, most importantly, a covering letter should be concise and ideally no more than three paragraphs long.

Ad: Right, a key point, would you agree, Aydin?

Ay: Yes, that's an ideal length. The letter needs to introduce you to the potential employer and state what you want to do for the employer.

Ad: Hans?

H: Let's not forget that the letter should also show how and why you are suited for that particular work.

S: Definitely.

Ad: Yes, Sophie? Please go on.

S: Another point you have to be careful about – the letter shouldn't be too long-winded. What's important here is to introduce yourself and to make an impact.

C: I completely agree. Impact is a key point. Employers are bombarded with a string of boring letters all written in the same format, don't you think, Hans?

H: Mm, to some extent you're right. It's important to get a balance; not to sound too dull on the one hand, but also not to sound over-confident.

Ad: That's a very good point, Hans. Your letter could discourage a potential employer if it comes across as too cocky. Anything we've missed?

T: Um, I think the obvious point we've missed is that the style of your letter is important. In my view, the key points are: one – the style of the covering letter should be reasonably formal and business-like; and two – it should match the CV or application form you're sending.

Ad: Good, anything else? … OK, Aydin.

Ay: Finally, one point nobody's mentioned is layout. Your letter should be typed using a clear font and on good-quality, plain white or cream paper, preferably the same as the CV. If you are e-mailing it, make it look business-like.

C: Exactly, and always write to a named individual, whether you are applying for a job or writing a speculative letter. If you don't know who to address the letter to, contact the company to find out the name of the relevant person. Make sure you check the spelling of their name; no one likes to have their name spelled incorrectly.

2.5

Let's look at the Statement of Financial Accounting Concepts No.2. This statement covers the qualitative characteristics of accounting information. The FASB, which is the principal accounting standard-setting body in the US, states that, in the end, each decision-maker personally decides what accounting information is useful. At the same time, that decision is influenced by several factors. These factors include, for example, the decisions to be made and the methods of decision-making to be used. Other factors are whether or not the information has already been obtained or can be obtained from other sources, and then of course there's the decision-maker's capacity to process the information. That is, can he or she process the information alone, or is professional help required?

---

3 Accounting systems

3.1

Speaker 1

Well, selecting accounting software is difficult. Personally, I always think that the software must be just the right size, it shouldn't contain more or fewer features than you need. Secondly, I believe that it's essential that you check the publisher will be able to provide upgrades and fix bugs when required. In my view, it's simply not enough to learn the package's specifications and understand its various features; at the same time, you must have both a clear, comprehensive understanding of your organization's business operations and the various processes that it uses.

3.2

Speaker 2

In my opinion, many people think that today's accounting software is so smart that it could be adapted to run any kind of business. This may be true to some extent, but I'm not convinced that it's the whole picture. Today's low-priced accounting software is 'smarter' and far more cost-effective than the most sophisticated packages of a generation ago. But nowadays, although price is still a significant factor, users expect their accounting software to do more than just bookkeeping. The latest packages come with sophisticated solutions and are capable of fully running a multitude of business processes. Additionally, since each software product has its own unique set of solutions, on top of basic bookkeeping – which is included in all accounting software – I think it's easy to understand why the search for the right product, one that matches solutions to your needs, is complicated.

3.3

Speaker 3

If you ask me, the search for accounting software is time-consuming; it often takes months of arduous research and evaluation. However, I feel that if you do the job carefully, you'll develop a panoramic picture of your organization that is far more comprehensive and detailed than you imagined. In the process, I'm sure you'll see how your various business processes combine with one another. In the long term, such insights will provide you with the opportunity to redesign processes that will make your business successful.

3.4

Speaker 1

The Professional Scheme is the primary qualification of the ACCA and allows you to become a Chartered Certified Accountant. For this, you will have to complete up to 14 professional examinations and complete three years of supervised, relevant accountancy experience. In accordance with ACCA's traditions, there is open access to its examinations. As part of the Professional Scheme, a Bachelor of Science (Honours) degree in Applied Accounting is offered in association with Oxford Brookes University. The degree is awarded after completing Part 2 of the Professional Scheme and submitting a research project.

3.5

Speaker 2

Moving on to the syllabus, the current syllabus is made up of 14 examinations, although some exemptions are available. The papers are divided into three parts. Within Part 3, there are four optional papers (of which two must be selected) and three core papers – these must be sat and passed together, subject to the referral rules.

The subjects examined include financial accounting, management accounting, financial audit, taxation, company law, financial management, management information systems and strategic management. Recently, some changes have been made to the syllabus. The new syllabus updates the qualification for recent developments in the accountancy profession and reorganizes the papers within the qualification. It is our policy to update the examination syllabus on a regular basis. Prior to the changes in 2007, changes were made previously in 2001 and 1994. The ACCA Professional examinations are offered worldwide twice yearly, in June and December.

3.6
Speaker 3
Another qualification you may decide to opt for is the CAT – the Certified Accounting Technician. This is actually an introductory accounting technician qualification. Although CAT can be obtained as a standalone qualification, many people often study for CAT as an introduction to accountancy prior to starting the Professional Scheme. It normally takes a year and a half to complete the Certified Accounting Technician exams. Currently, the CAT has been placed on the Qualifications and Curriculum Authority National Qualifications Framework, and publicly funded educational institutions are now eligible for funding to train towards the qualification in the UK.

3.7
Now let's move on to the next topic up for discussion – the issue of the international harmonization of accounting standards in the EU. As you all know, there have been endless heated debates on this topic. Since January 2005, all companies located in the European Union have had to use the accounting standards promulgated by the IASB. This means that, at a stroke, accounting standards for companies whose shares are listed on an EU stock exchange have been harmonized across 25 countries. As most of us would agree, this is certainly quite a tall order in terms of integrating Europe's financial markets and harmonizing accounting standards around the world. In fact, this situation raises two interesting questions. Firstly, why have accounting standards in the EU been harmonized? And secondly, why have IASB's standards been adopted, as opposed to other standards?

4 Company performance
4.1
In Singapore, following the recommendation of the Council on Corporate Disclosure and Governance, the Ministry of Finance decided to retain quarterly earnings reports for listed companies with a market capitalization of over 75 million Singapore dollars. The issue of mandatory quarterly reporting, which was introduced in 2003 for listed companies, has generated a heated discussion in the financial community. The Ministry has commented that, while it was aware of costs associated with quarterly reporting, on the other hand, the system was beneficial to the city-state's capital markets, as it promoted transparency and a high standard of disclosure. In fact, it is estimated that about 35% of all firms listed on the Singapore Exchange are required to report their results quarterly. In future, smaller companies will also be subject to a year-end review of their market caps. If they pass the 75-million-dollar threshold, they will be given a year to prepare themselves for quarterly reporting. On the other hand, bigger companies whose market caps dip below 75 million Singapore dollars will still have to continue with quarterly reports unless they get an exemption from the Singapore Exchange.

4.2
Extract 1
In 2007, the Big Four firms had an astounding total revenue of $89.2 billion. All four accounting firms had a banner year, with double-digit revenue growth on the heels of strong performances

in 2006 and 2005. KPMG had the highest annual growth rate among the firms with 17.4%, followed by Deloitte at 15.5%, Ernst and Young at 15% and PricewaterhouseCoopers bringing up the rear at 14.4%. Despite this relatively slower growth, PricewaterhouseCoopers remains the planet's largest accounting firm, with 2007 revenues of $25.2 billion, ahead of Deloitte at 23.1 billion, Ernst and Young at 21.1 billion, with KPMG being, relatively, the smallest firm at 19.8 billion. In my view, the firms will continue this level of strong performance, meaning another year of strong revenue growth in 2008. In this case, the combined total could easily exceed a hundred billion dollars.

4.3
Extract 2
As you know, the Big Four firms are inspected annually by the PCAOB, that is the Public Company Accounting Oversight Board. For three consecutive years now, the PCAOB has issued an annual report for each of these firms. Together, these four firms audit about 99 per cent of all public company revenues. The Big Four firms are Deloitte, Ernst and Young, KPMG and PricewaterhouseCoopers. Sadly, as was asserted in the 2007 inspection reports, the large accounting firms again had difficulty meeting the regulator's expectations. The PCAOB concluded that the Big Four firms had not gathered sufficient competent evidence to support the auditors' opinions issued with the Securities and Exchange Commission. The main problem with the giants' reporting was the number of audits with unsupported opinions. Although the results of the report are far from perfect, they were considerably better than the dreadful results identified in the first two reports conducted by the PCAOB in 2004 and 2005.

4.4
Good morning, ladies and gentlemen. This morning, I'd like to take a closer look at the outstanding performance noted in fund-management business in Hong Kong over the last few years. Firstly, 2005 was another year of record growth for fund-management business, with Hong Kong strengthening its position as a key financial centre of Asia.

An annual survey by the Securities and Futures Commission revealed that total asset size of the combined fund-management business in Hong Kong grew 25% to 4,526 billion Hong Kong dollars at the end of 2005. The figures show the fourth consecutive year of growth, which has surged to 54% in the last two years alone. This means that assets under management in Hong Kong have now nearly tripled since 2001.

I would like to emphasize here that these remarkable figures are the results of the professionalism, enterprise and hard work of Hong Kong fund managers and advisers. Other reasons include the facts that Hong Kong is a very accommodating place to set up a hedge fund, the regulatory environment is encouraging, and the support from lawyers, accountants, custodians and prime brokers is also strong.

Of the total non-REIT assets managed in Hong Kong, almost one-third – 28%, to be exact – was invested in Hong Kong and China. This further illustrates Hong Kong's position as the gateway to China, and the development of its expertise in managing investments in Asia.

The launch of Hong Kong's Real Estate Investment Trust market will further fuel the industry's growth spurt. Since November, four REITs managed by licensed corporations in Hong Kong have successfully launched and listed on the Hong Kong Stock Exchange, including the first product, Link REIT, the largest IPO of its kind in the world. By the end of June 2005, the total market capitalisation of the four REITs amounted to around 49 billion Hong Kong dollars, which is 6.3 million US dollars, with an average daily turnover of 373 million Hong Kong dollars, that is 47.8 million US dollars.

5 Auditing

5.1

Extract 1

Auditors spend considerable time interviewing client personnel. Yet most auditors have not received any formal training in the established principles of interviewing and how to plan and conduct an effective audit interview.

5.2

Extract 2

OK, well, as I see it, audit interviews are one of the most effective and efficient evidence-gathering procedures available to the auditor. By evidence-gathering, I mean 'method of obtaining evidence by asking questions, listening to and evaluating the responses and then asking appropriate follow-up questions'. Let me explain …

5.3

Extract 3

As you all know, in any interview, the type of question really dictates the quality of the answer. Professional interviewers know that a question's phrasing can significantly influence the response. The question 'We don't have a major inventory obsolescence problem, do we?' is biased, and will produce an entirely different response from the neutrally phrased question, 'How does the company identify potentially obsolete inventory items?'

5.4

Extract 4

Interview questions can be classified in two ways: firstly, whether the question is open-ended or closed, and secondly, whether the question is biased or unbiased; the openness of a question affects the likely range of responses. Open questions allow the interviewee to determine the range and scope of his or her response and to express it in his or her own terms.

5.5

Extract 5

Obviously, closed questions usually restrict the range of the interviewee's response to either 'yes' or 'no'. Therefore, at first, some may conclude an auditor should always ask open questions. However, each form of question has its particular strengths and is appropriate in different circumstances. Open questions provide greater information to the interviewer, but they also usually extend the length of the interview. Another drawback is that they also require greater interviewing expertise and are not appropriate when the auditor requires specific representations on an issue.

5.6

Extract 6

Finally, before I conclude my presentation this morning, I'd like to say a few words about biased questions. The bias of a question affects the validity of the responses. The auditor's objective in conducting an interview is to obtain valid, relevant evidentiary matter. Biased questions, in particular – so-called 'loaded questions' – produce neither valid nor relevant evidence.

5.7

Extract 7

What I'd really like to emphasize is that auditors should recognize how easy it is for bias to creep into interview questions, and that most people respond unconsciously to cues embedded in them. When conducting interviews, auditors should make deliberate, conscious attempts to phrase all questions in an unbiased manner. Indeed, the tendency to ask leading (and hence biased) questions is the most common error auditors make in conducting interviews.

5.8

Extract 8

Successful audit interviews begin with planning and preparation. Except for the shortest interview, the auditor should normally prepare a written agenda covering the topics to be discussed. This agenda will assist in asking questions during the interview and, just as important, assist in recalling what was said after the interview. Also, during the preparation process, the auditor should rehearse how particular questions will be phrased and make sure the phrasing does not bias the question.

5.9

Well, last year was a successful year for the internal audit recruitment market until the third quarter. The financial turmoil toward the end of the year left the market more subdued. This morning, I want to cover the main highlights of the recruitment market. Firstly, I'll provide you with some figures regarding the number of internal auditors employed. In the second part, I'll cover salary issues – namely, how salary increases have fallen to their lowest level for four years. Generally, internal audit recruitment amongst the Big Four was rather limited. The decline in Sarbanes-Oxley work that was particularly evident during the first half of 2007 resulted in a number of redundancies – not internal auditors, but principally contractors who had benefited from the previous boom. Demand from employers was primarily for manager-grade staff with financial services and banking experience. A number of the top-ten firms sought internal auditors with private-sector experience as they attempted to expand their services beyond the public sector. Within IT audit, candidates with project assurance and more broadly based skills in business processing were sought. However, there was little active recruitment in this area.

5.10

The interview is often the most challenging aspect of an audit for new auditors. Actually, the interview process may be the most important element of an audit. For that reason, auditors must be able to apply various techniques to gather as much information as possible. It's important to remember that all auditees are different. Some auditees may be familiar and comfortable with the audit interview, others may be nervous; hence the manner in which an auditor conducts the interview may determine the success of the interview. First and foremost, interviews should be relaxed and conversational. In my experience, the main mistake many auditors make is that they dive straight into the checklist. Instead, at the start of the interview, they should set aside some time for introductions. After a short time, the interview process will become more 'natural' and the interviewee will mention topics that are of interest to the auditor. At this point, the auditor can ask for more information and move on to the interviewee's position and duties. When the auditor uses a conversational process to conduct the audit, the interviewee, rather than the checklist, is the central figure. The auditor's focus should be to understand the process and the person's role in that process. Finally, auditors should use open-ended questions to elicit as much information as possible during the interview and ask follow-up questions to ensure understanding.

6 Ethics

6.1

Student 1

The AICPA Ethics Exam consists of 50 multiple-choice questions about different aspects of the AICPA Code of Professional Conduct. In order to qualify for licensing or certification, a score of at least 90% is required, so it's a pretty tall order. Personally, what I see as one of the main benefits on testing ethics through the new CPA Exam, as opposed to the separate AICPA Ethics Exam, is that it will achieve uniformity of ethical requirements in all states and can be designed to test analytical skills.

6.2

Student 2

Well, as I see it, a major weakness of the AICPA Ethics Exam is that it consists of only multiple-choice questions. My recommendation would be that, in future, consideration should be given to using alternative question formats in the exam in order to test more relevant skills and minimize the reliance upon memorization.

6.3

Student 3

Just as emphasizing ethics at the entrance to the profession helps fulfil accountants' public responsibility, emphasizing ethics through continuing education strengthens that commitment. Every state should consider requiring its CPAs to complete an ethics component as part of its mandatory CPE requirement. Changes should not be purely token, but should instead be pervasive throughout the accounting regulatory environment, starting with the education, testing and licensing of CPA candidates.

6.4

Student 4

I believe that, while the AICPA is making changes to the current CPA exam, it should also consider a substantial integration of ethics into the licensing requirements for CPAs. This can be done in a variety of ways, such as adding more questions on ethics to the CPA exam, testing about the subject through simulations, expanding the scope of coverage by integrating the subject into all test sections, and requiring candidates that have passed the CPA exam to take a separate ethics exam.

6.5

Student 5

The Sarbanes-Oxley Act and SAS 99 are simply not enough. My view is that steps must be taken at the gateway to the profession to provide accountants with a more substantial foundation in ethics. It is of the utmost importance that ethics is taught comprehensively, emphasized in the national exam, and subsequently included in the licensing process.

6.6

1	CPI	consumer price index
2	ARR	accounting rate of return
3	EMS	European monetary system
4	IRR	internal rate of return
5	IPO	initial public offering
6	SORP	statement of recommended practice
7	MMC	Monopolies and Mergers Commission
8	OFT	Office of Fair Trading
9	e&oe	errors and omissions excepted
10	RPM	resale price maintenance
11	PRDB	purchases returns day book

6.7

1 This is generally printed on an invoice and indicates that the business that has issued the invoice does not take any responsibility for any mistakes printed on the invoice.

2 This ratio measures the profit earned on an investment expressed as a percentage of the average investment. This method is often used to decide between alternative capital projects.

3 This is a book of prime entry; goods which have been returned to the supplier are entered here. It is compiled from credit notes received from the supplier.

6.8

Extract 1

Getting audited by the tax authorities is a nightmare scenario for anyone, no matter how meticulous and honest they are while preparing their tax return. However, if you think you have to be caught stashing away cash in an offshore bank account to trigger an audit, you should think twice. On today's programme, we are going to provide you with some assistance to avoid an audit by the tax authorities. But beware, just one tiny error on your tax returns, and you could have the tax man knocking on your door. In the USA in 2007, the IRS audited approximately 1.4 million returns, a 7% increase from 2006 and the highest number on record since 1998. My advice is that the best way to avoid an audit is to keep detailed records and retain receipts and bank statements that substantiate every claim, loss and deduction in your returns.

6.9

Extract 2

Right. Auditing for beginners. Where shall we start? Well, an audit can be compared to having an annual check-up with the doctor. Just as the patient must pass certain exams to ensure a clean bill of health, a company's financial 'good health' relies on whether or not its financial statements abide by generally acceptable standards and accounting principles. While the audit does not guarantee that the financial statement is perfect, it does provide a reasonable level of assurance that the statements are free of misstatements. So, in this case, the doctor is the auditor, and the company is the patient. Simple. Next, in order to judge financial statements, auditors use generally acceptable accounting principles, or GAAP. Basically, financial statements are considered to conform to the GAAP if the accounting principles used by management are generally accepted throughout the profession.

6.10

Extract 3

The major accounting institutes in the UK have urged the government to take action regarding who is permitted by law to describe themselves as an accountant. Representatives of the main accounting bodies have asked their members to help back a bid to legally define the term 'accountant'. The CCAB have for a long time been trying to persuade the government that people without proper qualifications should not be able to call themselves accountants. The accounting bodies are also currently researching cases in which members themselves have been called to a firm to rectify problems caused by a non-qualified accountant. The Department for Trade and Industry had previously said that the term 'chartered accountant' was recognized in legislation. The problem is that, under current legislation, anyone can call themselves an accountant without any qualifications, examinations or regulatory supervision.

7 Fraud

7.1

Speaker 1

As you know, the main topic today is fraud – frequently referred to as 'the unmanaged risk'. First of all, I'd like to show you why I think fraud is unmanaged. Then I'll demonstrate in what ways it's unmanaged. I also want to talk briefly about how I believe fraud can be detected. So, firstly, why do I believe that fraud is unmanaged?

7.2

Speaker 2

Last year, Ernst and Young sponsored a survey in which they asked the people who ought to know about fraud – the people who do it – whether or not they had in fact either done it or personally witnessed somebody who did. They surveyed a statistically legitimate sample of employees last year and asked them that very question: 'Have you stolen from your employer in the last 12 months, or if you haven't, have you personally witnessed somebody who has?' One in four of those people said 'yes' to that question. Now, that actually means that unless you happen to have fewer than four employees, you have almost certainly been a victim of fraud if you are an employer.

7.3

Speaker 3

Let me give you a few examples of fraud. Firstly, financial statement manipulation, where people actually modify records to make results look better. I suppose it's possible they could alter them to make them look worse, but that's not been my experience. Secondly, cases of people creating fictitious suppliers. Thirdly, claiming expenses that haven't been incurred.

7.4

Speaker 4

One of the main problems auditors face is that if you want to find fraud, you have to know what it looks like. I believe that's one of the fundamental reasons why audits are such poor tools for finding fraud – because most auditors don't know what fraud looks like. I've been in this business now for close to 20 years and I'm beginning to understand the scope and dimension of the problem. I don't have all of the solutions. This is not something that you can take a course on and be an expert in. But nor is it complicated.

7.5

Speaker 5

If you want to find fraud, you have to acknowledge some basic premises. First and foremost, you have to acknowledge that fraud happens a lot; it happens in your organization and mine – and in every organization around the world. So that's the first proposition: that it does happen and it happens a lot. Obviously fraud is hard to find because you're not supposed to find it. It's a deceptive activity; in fact, the whole point of fraud is that you don't find it. If people who committed fraud made it easy to find, then it wouldn't last very long.

7.6

The case involving the telecommunications tycoon – whose company, Eltek, employs over 3,000 staff – has been extensively covered in the Norwegian paper, *Drammens Tindende*, in recent weeks. The Norwegian owners of the Badenoch Estate in Scotland are being investigated for alleged tax fraud in their homeland. Mr and Mrs Angelil, whose official residence is now Cluny Estate, near Laggan, Scotland, are both facing charges of breaking tax laws in the Scandinavian country. The pair used to live in Norway before moving to the estate near Laggan in 2001. Concerns have been raised, however, that Mr and Mrs Angelil have been living in Norway tax-free for longer than is allowed by law. As a consequence, the court has seized the couple's summer cabin in Norway for 81.2 million Norwegian Kroner – around £750,000. The Angelils have been registered as living in Scotland since 2001, but remain regular visitors to Norway, where they still have family. It's believed that the Norwegian authorities have been investigating the amount of time the Angelils have spent living in their homeland tax-free over the last few years. During the first three years after registering for tax purposes as having moved abroad, an individual is not allowed to stay in Norway for more than 61 days per year. After that, the limit is 183 days. Any individual staying for longer than that will be considered by the Norwegian tax authorities to have returned home and be liable for payments.

Mr Angelil is also under investigation from the Norwegian Finance Fraud unit concerning insider trading of stocks with his brother. Before moving to Scotland, in the 1970s, Angelil established the Eltek company. Eltek has since grown to be an international company in the telecommunications industry, producing transmission systems and power solutions for wireless communication and mobile-phone services. Eltek was first noted on the Oslo Stock Exchange in 1998, and, at its peak in 2000, was worth more than 4 billion Norwegian Kroner. Today, the company is worth about 1.3 billion Norwegian Kroner, even after several acquisitions of other companies. The Angelil family controls around 15% of the shares in Eltek.

7.7

A bankrupt businessman, Peter Bradley, has admitted his part in a ten-million-pound scam which led to the collapse of a Merseyside gas company. His firm, Alta Gas, went into receivership in 2001 after a 40-million-pound hole was discovered in its accounts. The company employed 250 people at depots in Knowsley, Prenton, Garston and Bootle. Alta Gas's accounting problems were discovered in 2001, during investigations by a bank approached by the company for a loan to fund expansion plans. At the time, the firm's directors were seeking to raise 70 million pounds. Alta Gas's collapse and bankruptcy led to massive losses for several important financial companies, including Barclays Bank, which was owed 11.5 million pounds. Following the discovery of the massive accounting hole, the company was sold to Irish bottled-gas rival, Flogas. After the collapse of Alta Gas, Bradley went on the run, but was eventually arrested in 2006 in Mallorca by Spanish Serious Fraud officers after an international manhunt. Yesterday, Bradley was in Liverpool Crown Court faced with 36 charges involving at least ten million pounds, including counts of false accounting and fraudulent trading.

7.8

The US Securities and Exchange Commission has imposed an unusually heavy fine on McAlfie for an accounting scam between 1998 and 2000. The SEC stated that between 1998 and 2000, McAlfie overstated its revenues by 622 million dollars. In fact, for 1998 alone, revenues were hiked by 131 per cent, or 562 million dollars. In order to settle the embarrassing episode quickly, the company has agreed to pay 50 million dollars as punishment for the misstatements, though it has not formally admitted to the charges. The current management, which was not in any way involved or implicated in the fraud, has distanced itself from the scandal. A spokesman for the new management stated that this was an opportunity to reinforce the strong message of putting ethics first. A representative from the SEC, Roger Stone, commented that he hoped the heavy fine would act as a deterrent to using manipulative accounting practices for other public companies.

8 Banking

8.1

In the current climate of credit crunch, Britain's banks have been warned by the Financial Reporting Council that their balance sheets will be carefully scrutinized in future. The FRC is concerned that major financial institutions may attempt to hide the worst effects of the credit crunch. Auditors have also been warned to take extra care when checking the accounts of banks and other finance companies, before giving them a clean bill of health.

Of course, such warnings follow the global credit crunch, which has caused some of the world's largest banks to write off billions of pounds of assets. Investment banks UBS and Citigroup have sought billions in extra funds from the Middle East and Asia to strengthen their balance sheets. And we are all too familiar with the 25-billion-pound Bank of England rescue package for Northern Rock.

The FRC, which monitors company reporting and regulates the audit industry, has stressed that credit-market conditions mean that the risks to confidence in corporate reporting and governance are higher than they have been for several years. The watchdog also stated that increased risks require additional diligence.

8.2

What I like about *Accounting Standards for Central Banks* by James M. Koltveit is that is provides the straightforward, expert analysis necessary to guide accounting and banking professionals through the complex and numerous accounting rules unique to banks and financial institutions. In addition, the book features an array of examples, illustrations and many other valuable practice aids for any special situations that may be encountered. Two other essential features of the book are that it explains how to analyze a bank's financial position and operations using the bank's financial statements, and discusses the accounting principles applicable to banks within the framework of their operations. *Accounting Standards for Central Banks* aims to offer an insight into key debates and emerging best practice in central-bank financial reporting. It brings together in one volume contributions from leading international experts, not only first-hand practitioners from central banks themselves, but also experts from standard-setting international institutions. In a nutshell, the book is a goldmine of information for anyone who requires an overview of central-banking reporting.

8.3
Speaker 1
The movement towards fair-value accounting has been undertaken without evidence that the valuations produced are actually 'better' than the old valuations, and if you ask me, this approach is nonsense. In contrast, I think that recent evidence indicates that use of fair valuation has the potential for spectacularly misleading results.

8.4
Speaker 2
There is no doubt that the new regulations and requirements have increased demand for compliance professionals. Both local corporations and multinationals are strengthening their control and compliance functions, and the Big Four accountancy firms are having to battle hard to retain staff who are offered attractive incentives to move elsewhere. I am keen to recruit a team of candidates who are technically sound and understand the importance of applying the appropriate laws and regulations.

8.5
Speaker 3
I believe there are many obstacles facing graduate accountancy professionals as they emerge from the classroom into the corporate world. Somehow, there is a myth that accountancy degrees guarantee great wages and job stability, but in my experience so far, this has certainly been far from the truth. Personally, I have seen the competition expand from local to international applicants for graduate accountancy jobs. The use of online job websites, along with virtual meetings and interviews, means that firms can speak to a candidate from the other side of the world without much trouble, which means your application and CV need to explain why you are the best person for a position.

9 Insurance
9.1
Right, ladies and gentlemen, shall we get started? In my presentation this morning, I would like to touch on three subjects. First, I want to argue that the increasing blurring of the boundaries between insurance and other financial institutions in my view implies a heightened importance of the insurance industry for systemic financial stability, and calls for a stronger supervisory focus on financial risks (as opposed to underwriting risks). I am totally convinced that more disclosure and transparency of financial risks and how they are managed is also becoming increasingly necessary.

Second, I want to highlight that fair-value accounting, if properly implemented, will likely make more explicit the redistribution of risks over time that is being done by insurers. I tend to think that this will occur almost as a by-product of their core business of risk-pooling, and could improve the pricing of those risks.

Third, as the arguments in the vigorous debate on fair-value accounting appear rather entrenched, I feel we need to search for a middle ground on this issue: methods that might address some of the problems associated with fair-value accounting, while retaining most of the benefits, particularly improved transparency and consistency of financial statements.

9.2
Six years ago, we were working for a larger, national accounting firm and really felt that some of our clients didn't seem to be served by our company's business model. We felt their basic needs weren't being met, and my partner and I were fortunate enough to be able to negotiate a friendly buyout with our employer. This meant we were able to take 40 of our clients with us. We then founded Strohm Ballweg LLP in Madison. Though the company had a most humble beginning – it actually started off in my dining room – it has now grown to three partners and 15 employees. During the past four years, we have averaged 24% growth, and our client roster has grown from the initial 40 to more than 75. We took a risk when we decided to focus on the insurance industry. Nowadays, we operate a public-accounting firm that concentrates almost exclusively on providing accounting services to the insurance industry. Our focus is on providing auditing and tax services, regulatory filing and other back-office services.

9.3
In fact, the state exercises greater supervision over insurance than many other activities. This is because the economic and social purpose of insurance is the transfer of risk from the policyholder to the insurer. If an insurance company fails, then the object of this transfer of risk is not achieved. While a buyer of goods or services will usually know very quickly if a trader is unable to supply the goods or services promised, a buyer of insurance will not know whether a claim can be met until it arises. Even if a company is financially sound when the policyholder pays the premium, the situation may have altered by the time a claim arises through, for example, mismanagement or even misconduct. An insolvent insurance company would leave its policyholders exposed to claims which the company may not be able to meet.

The regulatory legislation in this area aims firstly to prevent insurers getting into difficulties by laying down authorization, solvency and reporting requirements. If prevention fails, policyholder-protection legislation provides a mechanism for the policyholders of insolvent insurance companies to be covered through a guarantee fund in certain circumstances.

In the UK, responsibility for supervision of general insurance business lay with the Insurance Division of the Department of Trade and Industry until 1997. It was then transferred to the Treasury, although most of the day-to-day regulatory functions were delegated to the Financial Services Authority, before the FSA took full responsibility for regulation in 2001.

10 Bankruptcy
10.1
Today, the American business and financial communities are preoccupied as seldom before with the consequences of a flurry of investigations into allegations of corporate wrongdoing. The 'Hall of Shame' of significant American businesses involved in these proceedings now includes the likes of Enron, WorldCom, Tyco, Adelphia, Global Crossing and HealthSouth – all discredited by illegalities or improper accounting practices. Numerous members of the management teams of these companies have had to face criminal prosecution or regulatory sanctions that have effectively ended their careers. Meanwhile, the venerable accounting firm of Arthur Andersen, once the cream of the accounting profession, has been forced from the field, and more investigations appear to be on the cards. The spate of corporate scandals which we must deal with today is not unique. It is only the latest of those which have, from time to time, posed threats to our free enterprise system and its long-established record of efficient allocation of resources within our economy. Nonetheless, these episodes have had

significant consequences on the American business and financial communities. Indeed, some have suggested that these breakdowns have created a true crisis in corporate America – a proposition which I propose to cover this evening.

10.2

I would like to share with you some specific insights gained from my own service as the court-appointed examiner in the largest bankruptcy proceedings in American history. WorldCom, the world's second largest telecommunications company, filed for bankruptcy in the federal court in Manhattan in the summer of 2002, after the disclosure of massive accounting irregularities. I was appointed as examiner by the bankruptcy court in August 2002, filed my first interim report that November, a second interim report in June of 2003 and my final report in early 2004. The WorldCom case has gripped the nation's attention as it has become a kind of 'poster child' for corporate governance failures this century. My remarks tonight will only cover the results of our completed investigations which have been made public. But even the public story provides a genuine case study in the failure of corporate governance and suggests a number of lessons in how to avoid its repetition.

10.3

Some of you may be wondering what a bankruptcy examiner is and what exactly one does. Well, simply put, a bankruptcy examiner is appointed by the judge of the Bankruptcy Court to carry out an independent investigation into a case and to establish what happened. So, in the WorldCom case, my job was to assure the judge that procedures and persons involved in any past wrongdoing were not carried forward into the reorganized entity. We were also asked to identify potential courses of action that the company might have against third parties responsible for losses to the company and to make recommendations to aid in avoiding repetition elsewhere of the acts that caused the downfall of WorldCom. We worked closely with the US Department of Justice and state prosecutors, although we had no criminal jurisdiction. We also worked with the SEC and other regulators, although we had no regulatory responsibility. And we worked with representatives of the creditors of the company and the Corporate Monitor appointed in connection with the SEC proceedings to fully develop the facts. Our completed reports are now in the hands of the public and the new management of WorldCom for their guidance.

10.4

Speaker 1

If you live in the UK and have debt or financial problems, you have probably noticed the flood of television advertisements from debt-management or debt-consolidation companies. As a result of the increasing debt totals of consumers, there are now over 600 commercial companies in the debt industry. Most debt-management companies in the UK spend thousands of pounds each week advertising their services. The end result is that these companies must recoup this investment through charging exorbitant fees. Unfortunately, due to the prevalence of such debt-management company ads, thousands of people sign up with them. In many cases, consumers do not realize the extent of the payments and fees these companies charge. Many consumers have started out with a debt-consolidation or management company and ended up more in debt than when they began. The Insolvency Helpline estimates that up to 70% of its clients have had previous problems with debt-consolidation companies. Invariably, if financial problems are addressed at an earlier stage, there are much simpler solutions.

10.5

Speaker 2

The Insolvency Helpline is the largest professional network providing debt and money advice. Formed in 1997, it provides debt advice and support to both individual consumers and businesses. This consultancy network is composed of professional accountants and lawyers and receives over one million calls per year. The aim of the Helpline is to promote the provision of independent money advice from professional bodies in the UK. Besides its general advisory services, the Insolvency Helpline has established Divorceaid, a nonprofit group which sponsors a specialized programme, 'Debts and divorce', to assist those who are going through a divorce and having financial problems. With over 160,000 divorces per year in the UK, a survey found that 45% of divorcing or divorced people experienced financial problems, of which 36% were heavily in debt.

10.6

Speaker 3

The Insolvency Helpline offers a wide variety of financial-oriented services to consumers and businesses through its 24-hour phone line. It offers debt counselling and advice via the phone or through its interactive online service. Specific services include basic debt counselling and information, Individual Voluntary Agreements, Administration Orders, and debt-management advice and support. One area in which there is a great demand for assistance is mortgage and remortgage information and support. In addition, it provides bankruptcy information and advice, and a great deal of self-help information for consumers, such as a do-it-yourself online financial statement and sample letters to creditors.

10.7

Speaker 4

The rate of consumer debt in the UK has reached a record high. It is estimated that approximately two million people in the UK have unsecured debts in excess of £10,000. There are a number of causes for this problem, including job loss, health problems, divorce and poor money management. In one survey by PricewaterhouseCoopers, it was determined that of the insolvencies they studied in 2005, 75% were due to people living beyond their means. This is not a total surprise when you consider the ease of obtaining and using credit cards. Many credit-card suppliers don't even do a credit check on borrowers before offering the cards. Interest rates on some of these credit cards can also be incredibly high. For instance, the Vanquis Bank Card, from the Provident Financial Group, charges an unbelievable 69.5% APR, in addition to an annual fee.

10.8

Speaker 5

When you talk to someone on the Insolvency Helpline, you can be sure that you're getting good advice. Firms that provide advice through the Insolvency Helpline are all members of recognized professional associations such as the Insolvency Practitioners Association, the Association of Business Recovery Professionals or the Association of Chartered Certified Accountants. Another advantage is that the helpline is totally independent of any financial institution or group and is funded by donations and subscriptions of member professional firms. This means advice and counselling is provided free of charge and is generally available immediately. Obviously, all information received and provided is kept completely confidential.

Answer key

1 Introduction to ICFE

Reading
Skills
2 1 scandal 2 concern 3 untrue 4 necessary 5 covered
6 sentenced
3 1 in 2 its 3 has 4 As 5 Basically 6 Although
7 could/can 8 your/the 9 completely/very 10 Therefore
11 but 12 However

Exam focus
1 1 formation 2 statement 3 promulgated 4 announcement
5 description 6 arrangement(s)
2 1 D 2 A 3 B 4 D 5 C 6 A 7 D
3 1 E 2 F 3 A 4 C 5 B
Sentence D does not fit any of the gaps.

Listening
Skills
1 1 False. Pacioli wrote *Summa*, considered to be the first
'textbook', in 1494.
2 True
3 True
4 False. Evidence suggests that double-entry bookkeeping was
an invention of Italian merchants in the
Genoa–Venice–Florence triangle in the period 1200–1350.
5 True
6 True
7 False. The 'modern' cost-accounting system used by
industrial giants was developed by Donaldson Brown, the
CFO of General Motors, in 1920.
8 True. Amatino Manucci wrote the earliest surviving
complete double-entry bookkeeping system.
2 B
3 1 the business centre of Europe
2 'the father of accounting'
3 a mathematician
4 Leonardo da Vinci
5 all the mathematics known at that time
6 double-entry accounting
7 be used to prove a balanced ledger
8 the certification of books and cost accounting

Exam focus
2 Task One: 1 F 2 D 3 A 4 C 5 B
(Reason E is not mentioned.)
Task Two: 1 B 2 F 3 A 4 E 5 C
(Benefit D is not mentioned.)

Writing
Exam focus
2 *Suggested answer*
Report
Subject: Outsourcing of management accounting and payroll
Management accounts are the primary source of information
which businesses and organizations use to run their operations
and plan for the future. However, many small and medium-
sized businesses do not have the necessary in-house resources or
capabilities to produce this invaluable source of management
information.

Handing over the task of preparing management accounts to
our firm will not only provide you with improved quality of
financial reporting and management information, but at the
same time, you will be confident that you are fully compliant
with the relevant financial reporting standards and regulations.

Additionally, we can help to improve your finance staff's
knowledge of the key aspects of financial reporting standards.
Although the main aim of management accounts is to provide
an accurate picture of business and financial performance, we
can tailor the report to match your specific needs. For example,
we can incorporate actual performance versus budgeted
performance, cash projections and key performance indicators.
Processing payroll in-house is another activity which requires a
significant investment of employee time and can prove costly.
Even the most experienced finance and HR professionals would
agree that dealing with payroll can be a headache. Outsourcing
payroll is an affordable way for many businesses to remove the
complications. We can provide you with a fully managed
outsourced payroll service. We also provide payroll
healthchecks, to ensure that your payroll processes, procedures,
systems and tax calculations are efficient, reliable and compliant
with legal and statutory obligations.
(247 words)

2 The financial environment

Reading
Skills
1 1 d 2 a 3 b 4 i 5 h 6 g 7 f 8 c 9 e
2 1 framework 2 concepts 3 compiled 4 external 5 resolving
6 highlights 7 issues 8 pronouncements 9 adopted
Exam focus
1 1 range 2 assume 3 aim 4 expertise 5 insolvency 6 solid
2 1 A 2 B 3 D 4 B 5 B 6 C

Listening
Skills
1 a 1854 b 34%, 56%, 66%, 94% c 2,400, 16,000 d 94%
2 a 1854: ICAS was founded
b 56% of ICAS members work in industry/commerce
66% of students are based in England
34% are based in Scotland,
94% of graduates recruited possess a first- or upper-second-
class honours degree
c 2,400: the total number of students in the UK
16,000: members worldwide
d 94%: growth rate of ICAS
3 1 … tell you what makes ICAS stand out from other
professional bodies of accountants.
2 … professional body of accountants in the world.
3 … the fastest-growing accountancy body in the UK.
4 Requirements for training as a CA: You must secure a training
contract with an organization authorized by ICAS.
No. of training vacancies (UK): over 1,000
Employers are looking for a strong academic performance, both
at school and university.
Exemptions from exams: Depending on the relevance of your
degree subject, you can be exempt from some of the five exams
at Test of Competence.

Exam focus
1 B
2 1 Sophie 2 Aydin 3 Chanelle 4 Tony 5 Hans
3 1 B 2 B 3 A 4 B 5 C 6 A
4 1 The qualitative characteristics of accounting information
2 To set accounting standards in the USA

3 ... that judgement is influenced by factors such as the decisions to be made, the methods of decision-making to be applied, the information already possessed or obtainable from other sources and the decision-maker's capacity to process the information.

4 Can he or she process the information alone, or is professional help required?

Writing

Skills

1 1 introduction   2 introduction   3 conclusion   4 introduction
  5 conclusion   6 introduction   7 introduction   8 conclusion
  9 conclusion   10 conclusion   11 conclusion   12 conclusion
  Sentences 5, 9 and 12 are informal.

2 *Suggested answers*

1 I am writing in reponse to your correspondence regarding Ecofarms Limited and would like to confirm that Dee & Hall have recently been appointed to act as the firm's accountants.

2 Further to your advertisement for the position of accountant, which appeared in *Financial World*, I am writing to apply for this position.

3 I am writing to inform you that I have been appointed to audit the consolidated financial statements of Redgrove Care Limited.

4 The purpose of my letter is to confirm receipt of your invitation to attend an interview at the University of Brighton at 10.30 a.m. on Friday 10th April.

3/4 *Suggested answer*

Dear Mrs Harris,

I **am writing to** apply for the position of Chief Accountant, **which was** advertised in the *Financial Times*, **on the 3rd of** January, 2008.

I currently **hold** a senior accountant position with full responsibility for the monthly profit-and-loss statement of ~~the~~ Infinity Foods Limited. **I would also like to point out that** the last five years of my accounting experience has ~~always~~ been with the food industry.

I enclose a copy of my CV **and would be delighted to discuss my suitability for this position at** an interview.

Yours sincerely,

Enclosure: CV

---

3 Accounting systems

Reading

Skills

1 1 F   2 C   3 H   4 D   5 B   6 G   7 E   8 A

2 B, C, E, D, F, A

5 1 the development capability of the package
  2 use the product's in-built development tools
  3 required many months of programming
  4 upgrade to new versions of the software
  5 easier to use and allow the customers to upgrade to new product releases whilst retaining the developed features along the way
  6 development tools that allow developers to tailor the system to meet their client's needs more fully
  7 to evaluate the software's development capabilities before making your selection

Exam focus

1 consider   2 development capability   3 designed   4 adapt
5 needs   6 amended   7 adopted   8 sectors   9 source codes
10 time-consuming   11 with   12 versions   13 user-friendly
14 upgrade   15 strategy   16 development tools   17 evaluate

Listening

Skills

1 difficult, essential, comprehensive, smart, cost-effective, sophisticated, capable, unique, easy, complicated, time-consuming, arduous, panoramic, detailed, successful

2 1 Speaker 1   2 Speaker 1   3 Speaker 2   4 Speaker 3
  5 Speaker 1   6 Speaker 2   7 Speaker 3   8 Speaker 3
  9 Speaker 1

3 1 A, C   2 B, D   3 C, D

Exam focus

1 1 a Chartered Certified Accountant.
  2 supervised, relevant accountancy experience.
  3 Part 2 of the Professional Scheme and submitting a research project.
  4 pass three core papers, which must be sat and passed together, subject to the referral rules.
  5 to update the qualification for recent developments in the accountancy profession and reorganize the papers within the qualification.
  6 worldwide twice yearly, in June and December.
  7 an introduction to accountancy prior to starting the Professional Scheme.
  8 Qualifications and Curriculum Authority (QCA) National Qualifications Framework.
  9 publicly funded educational institutions.

3 1 The issue of the international harmonization of accounting standards in the EU
  2 All companies located in the European Union have had to use the accounting standards promulgated by the IASB
  3 They have been harmonized across 25 countries.
  4 a Why have accounting standards in the EU been harmonized?
    b Why have IASB's standards being adopted as opposed to other standards?

4 1 harmonization   2 promulgated   3 listed   4 integration
  5 adopted

Writing

Skills

1 *Suggested answer*
  1, 3, 5, 6, 9

2 1 d   2 b   3 f   4 e   5 g   6 c   7 h   8 a

Exam focus

1 1 e   2 i   3 f   4 a   5 g   6 c   7 j   8 d   9 b   10 h

2 *Suggested answer*

The purpose of this letter is to introduce Thomas Forman, whose personal details and signature appear below, to the ICAEW and to apply for his permission to use the ICAEW library facilities under my sponsorship.

I confirm that I have known Thomas personally since 1995. I would also like to point out that he is a serious reader whose professional/academic qualifications are appropriate to make use of the library facilities.

He is currently researching training courses for forensic accountants, focusing on preventative measures, and will spend the next six months in London writing his dissertation. I would therefore be grateful if you would allow him to use the ICAEW library facilities until September this year.

I hereby undertake to indemnify the Library against any loss or damage resulting from his/her use of the Library facilities under my sponsorship. I myself have been a member of the ICAEW since 1985.

I look forward to hearing from you.

(156 words)

4 Company performance

Reading

Skills

1 1 transactions 2 relationships 3 bookkeeping 4 entries
5 debit 6 credit 7 errors 8 practices 9 reform 10 assets
11 principles 12 measures

2 a *Suggested answers*
1 A name and information about that person?
2 General information about growth in BRIC countries?
3 Other alternatives?
4 Details about other countries with growth potential/high risk level?
5 Further comment(s) on growth of emerging economies/OECD?
b 1 C 2 E 3 D 4 F 5 B

Exam focus

1 1 who 2 for 3 provided/supplied 4 done
5 delivering/sending 6 terms 7 date 8 simple 9 can
10 up 11 company's 12 owe 13 classified/classed

2 1 computation 2 liabilities 3 accrual 4 subsidiaries
5 estimation 6 reported 7 disclosure

3 1 snapshot 2 condition 3 income 4 expenditure 5 held
6 covered 7 accrued 8 dues 9 flow 10 monies
11 collected 12 value

Listening

Skills

1 1 c 2 b 3 g 4 h 5 f 6 a 7 e 8 d

2 1 $75m 2 35% 3 S$75m

3 1 To retain quarterly earnings reports for listed companies.
2 To retain quarterly earnings reports for listed companies with a market capitalization of over S$75m.
3 It generated a heated discussion.
4 Extra costs associated with quarterly reporting
5 The system was beneficial to the city-state's capital markets.
6 Smaller companies will also be subject to a year-end review of their market caps.

Exam focus

1 1 A 2 C 3 B 4 A

2 1 key financial centre 2 total asset size 3 nearly tripled
4 fund managers 5 very accommodating place
6 prime brokers 7 was invested 8 largest IPO
9 average daily turnover

Writing

Exam focus

2 1 with 2 in 3 by 4 since 5 thereby 6 to 7 how 8 such
9 nor 10 an 11 both 12 for 13 This 14 The 15 made
16 at 17 further 18 of

5 Auditing

Reading

Skills

1 1 result 2 evaluation 3 entity 4 auditee 5 user
6 government 7 tool 8 business 9 information
10 investors

2 1 In America's Prohibition days.
2 Al Capone
3 Governmental entities, the IRS, the Federal Bureau of Investigation, state and local police departments.
4 Reviews evidence, conducts analyses, interviews involved parties and draws conclusions.
5 Standardized methodologies and practices found in many other professions.
6 After an alleged fraud has taken place.

3 1 F 2 B 3 A 4 E 5 C
Sentence D is not used.

Exam focus

1 1 C 2 D 3 E 4 A 5 B

2 1 for instance 2 in accordance with 3 In addition
4 subsequently 5 Furthermore

3 1 C 2 D 3 A 4 B 5 D 6 C 7 B 8 A 9 C 10 D 11 B
12 C

Listening

Skills

1 *Suggested answers*
1 Training in interview techniques
2 Open questions are more effective.
3 Using closed or biased questions.

2 1 run through 2 proof 3 loaded 4 out of date 5 classify
6 expertise

3 1 G 2 E 3 H 4 D 5 F 6 B 7 C 8 A

Exam focus

1 1 B 2 B 3 C 4 A 5 C 6 A

2 1 The interview
2 Apply various techniques
3 Some will be familiar and comfortable with the audit process, others may be nervous.
4 It should be relaxed and conversational.
5 They dive straight into the checklist.
6 Set aside time for introductions
7 Natural
8 The interviewee
9 To understand the process and the person's role in that process.
10 Open-ended / follow-up

3 *Suggested answer*
For new auditors, the most difficult aspect of an audit is the interview. In order to glean as much information as possible, it is advisable to use varied interviewing techniques. Another crucial point is that, as some interviewees are nervous of the interview process, the interview should be relaxed and conversational. Despite this, many auditors make the mistake of immediately tackling their checklist, instead of allowing the interview to proceed in a more natural way. Auditors should remember that the interviewee is the central figure in the interview; hence, they should concentrate on understanding both the interview process and the interviewee's role in that process. Finally, the auditor should use open questions and follow-up questions to check his/her comprehension.
(119 words)

Writing

Skills

1 Recently, credit-rating agencies **were** sharply criticized for failing to **recognize** the risks in hundreds of billions worth of mortgage-backed securities, **whose** values continue to plummet as home-loan defaults grow. The Treasury, the SEC and several congressional committees are now investigating why credit-rating agencies such as Standard and Poors, Moody's, and Fitch gave **endorsed** securities backed by sub-prime mortgages **after** downgrading them only in July.
The real mystery is why this issue **is** to be investigated. It's obvious why credit-rating agencies didn't blow the whistle. They didn't blow the whistle on Enron **or** WorldCom before those entities collapsed, either. You see, credit-rating agencies are paid by **the** same institutions that package and **sell** the securities the agencies are rating. If **an** investment bank doesn't like the rating, it doesn't have to pay it. And even if it likes the rating, **it** pays only after the security is sold. It's as if movie studios hired film critics to review their movies, and paid them only if the reviews were positive enough to get lots of people to see a movie.

Until the recent **collapse**, the results **were** great for credit-rating agencies. Profits at Moody's more than doubled between 2002 and 2006. And it was a great ride for the issuers of mortgage-backed securities. Demand soared due to the high ratings **and** expanded the market. Traders that bought, rebundled, and then sold them didn't have to **examine** anything except the ratings. It was actually a market in credit ratings – a multi-billion-dollar game of musical chairs. Then the music stopped.

2 1 C   2 D   3 D   4 A   5 C   6 D   7 A   8 B   9 C   10 B   11 D   12 B

Exam focus

1 *Suggested answers*

1 A common debate in the accounting profession is whether or not accrual accounting really provides the benefits which are claimed for it. The accrual principle may be called 'the mother of all accounting principles'. It ensures that revenues and expenses are recorded when earned and incurred and not necessarily when cash is exchanged. One of the arguments in favour of accrual accounting is that it measures current income more accurately than the cash method. On the other hand, it can be said that accrual accounting is difficult to understand. This report outlines some of the main advantages of accrual accounting and provides examples.

2 Managing the accounting tasks of any company is not an easy job; it can be costly and requires a great deal of resources. Hence, many companies are now opting for outsourced accounting. In my opinion, one of the main advantages of outsourced accounting is that it gives a company access to an expert accounting team and sophisticated accounting systems without having to invest vast amounts to establish an accounting department. Moreover, with the aid of outsourced accounting, any business owner, as well as his/her employees, is able to get a clear picture of the business in terms of profits earned and losses incurred. However, it is essential that the management fully understands the mechanism of outsourced accounting in order to benefit from its services and facilities. It is also important to consider the disadvantages of handing over the responsibility of dealing with all aspects of accounting to an external party.

3 In order to avoid misunderstandings of the results of accounting, many efforts are being made to harmonize auditing standards. Personally, I believe that efforts to harmonize standards should at the same time defend local, differing, standards and defend the right of individual auditors to exercise their own professional judgement. In this report, I will outline my views on the main advantages and disadvantages of the harmonization of accounting standards.

2 *Suggested answer*

The primary functions of an internal auditing department are to determine that internal systems and controls are adequate and effective, to ensure that institutional policies and procedures, appropriate laws and good business practices are followed, and to evaluate the adequacy and reliability of information available for management decisions. The task of internal auditing differs from that of external auditing, as it is determined by the organization itself, and its goals differ from those of the external auditor, who is appointed to report independently.

The independent auditor views internal control in terms of an entity's true and fair preparation and presentation of the financial statements, but does not express an opinion on the effectiveness of the entity's overall internal controls.

One benefit of having an internal auditing department is that it dispenses with the need to employ external consultants as internal auditors, hence saving large sums of money. Secondly, a separate internal auditing department enables a firm to constantly review management accounting of the company. At the same time, it ensures that the organization's standard policy

and procedures are running smoothly. As the internal auditors are well acquainted with the business and have access to a lot of confidential information and to all levels of management, they have very in-depth knowledge, which they can then contribute to the company.

Finally, the internal audit can be beneficial to most organizations because it provides management with a methodology to identify the risks that may prevent the organization from meeting its objectives.

6 Ethics

Reading

Skills

2 1 C   2 E   3 D   4 G   5 F   6 B   7 A
3 1 f   2 d   3 a   4 e   5 b   6 c
4 1 noun: *decisions*   2 adjective: *truthful*   3 adjective: *ethical*
4 noun: *code*   5 verb: *adhere*   6 noun: *balances*   7 adjective: *vital*
8 noun: *accountant*   9 verb: *should/must*   10 verb: *rely*
11 noun: *life*   12 verb: *(en)trusting*

Exam focus

1 1 C   2 G   3 E   4 B   5 A   6 D
Sentence F is not used.

2 1 regulatory   2 deteriorated   3 legislation   4 attestation
5 penalties   6 issuers   7 representations   8 accuracy
9 Consideration   10 detection

Listening

Skills

1 *Suggested answers*

1 The American Institute of Certified Public Accountants is the national, professional organization for all certified public accountants.

2 The Sarbanes-Oxley Act came into effect on 30 July 2002, and introduced highly significant legislative changes to financial practice and corporate governance regulation. It introduced stringent new rules with the stated objective 'to protect investors by improving the accuracy and reliability of corporate disclosures made pursuant to the securities laws'.

3 SAS 99 stands for Statement on Auditing Standards No.99. *Consideration of Fraud in a Financial Statement Audit* is an auditing statement issued by the Auditing Standards Board of the American Institute of Certified Public Accountants (AICPA). SAS 99 became effective for audits of financial statements for periods beginning on or after 15 December 2002 and was issued partly in response to accounting scandals such as Enron.

4 CPA (Certified Public Accountant) is the title of qualified accountants in the USA who have passed the Uniform Certified Public Accountant Examination and have met additional state education and experience requirements for certification as a CPA.

2 **Recommendations**

Speaker 2: My recommendation would be that, in future, consideration should be given to using alternative question formats on the exam in order to test more relevant skills and minimize the reliance upon memorization.

Speaker 3: Every state should consider requiring its CPAs to complete an ethics component as part of its mandatory CPE requirement.

Speaker 4: I believe that, while the AICPA is making changes to the current CPA exam, it should also consider a substantial integration of ethics into the licensing requirements for CPAs.

Speaker 5: My view is that steps must be taken at the gateway to the profession to provide accountants with a more substantial foundation in ethics.

Benefits

Speaker 1: Personally, what I see as one of the main benefits on testing ethics through the new CPA Exam [...] is that it will achieve uniformity of ethical requirements in all states and can be designed to test analytical skills.

Weaknesses

Speaker 1: ... a score of at least 90% is required, so it's a pretty tall order.

Speaker 2: ... a major weakness of the AICPA Ethics Exam is that it consists of only multiple-choice questions.

Speaker 5: The Sarbanes-Oxley Act and SAS 99 are simply not enough.

Exam focus

1 1 CPI   consumer price index
   2 ARR   accounting rate of return
   3 EMS   European monetary system
   4 IRR   internal rate of return
   5 IPO   initial public offering
   6 SORP   statement of recommended practice
   7 MMC   Monopolies and Mergers Commission
   8 OFT   Office of Fair Trading
   9 e&oe   errors and omissions excepted
  10 RPM   resale price maintenance
  11 PRDB   purchases returns day book

2 1 e&oe   2 ARR   3 PRDB

3 1 A   2 C   3 B   4 C   5 B   6 A

Writing

Exam focus

1 §1: 1 C   §2: 2 A, 3 F   §3: 4 B, 5 E, 6 G, 7 D

2 *Suggested answer*

We have audited the parent company financial statements of Crystal Group plc for the year ended 1 July 2007, which comprise the Company Balance Sheet and the related notes. The directors are responsible for preparing the Annual Report and the parent company financial statements in accordance with applicable United Kingdom law and Accounting Standards (United Kingdom Generally Accepted Accounting Practice) as set out in the Statement of Directors' Responsibilities. Our responsibility is to audit the parent company financial statements in accordance with relevant legal and regulatory requirements and International Standards on Auditing (UK and Ireland).

We conducted our audit in accordance with International Standards on Auditing (UK and Ireland) issued by the Auditing Practices Board. An audit includes examination, on a test basis, of evidence relevant to the amounts and disclosures in the parent company financial statements to be audited. It also includes an assessment of the significant estimates and judgements made by the directors in the preparation of the parent company financial statements, and of whether the accounting policies are appropriate to the company's circumstances, consistently applied and adequately disclosed. In forming our opinion, we also evaluated the overall adequacy of the presentation of information in the parent company financial statements to be audited.

In our opinion, the parent company financial statements give a true and fair view, in accordance with United Kingdom Generally Accepted Accounting Practice, of the state of the company's affairs as at 1 July 2007.

(240 words)

7 Fraud

Reading

Skills

1 1 d   2 a   3 c   4 h   5 b   6 i   7 f   8 e   9 j   10 k   11 g

2 1 D   2 E   3 C   4 A   5 F   6 B

3 1 ... Andersen was convicted of obstruction of justice for shredding documents connected to its audit of Enron.
   2 Since convicted felons are not permitted to audit public companies, the firm agreed to surrender its licences and its right to practise ...
   3 ... the Supreme Court of the United States unanimously overturned Andersen's conviction as a result of flaws in jury instructions.
   4 ... it is highly unlikely Andersen will ever return as a viable business.
   5 ... there are still over 100 civil suits pending against Arthur Andersen ...
   6 ... the firm has been reduced to around 200 [employees] ...

4 1 felony   2 obstruction   3 conspiracy   4 prosecution
   5 ruling   6 Fraudulent

Exam focus

1 1 Amendment   2 seizure   3 fraudulent   4 obstruction
   5 investment   6 conspiracy   7 convicted   8 prosecution
   9 permitted   10 annulled

2 1 C   2 E   3 F   4 A   5 G   6 B   7 H
Sentence D does not belong to any of the paragraphs.

Listening

Skills

1 1 G, K   2 D, J   3 C, F   4 A, B   5 E, H
Topic I is not covered.

2 1 Why do I believe that fraud is unmanaged?
   2 A sample of employees; one in four of the sample had committed fraud.
   3 Financial statement manipulation; creating ficticious suppliers; charging expenses that were not incurred for personal benefit
   4 It is difficult to know what it looks like.
   5 Fraud happens a lot and it happens everywhere.

Exam focus

2 1 alleged tax fraud   2 face charges   3 has seized
   4 for tax purposes   5 considered   6 insider trading
   7 in the 1970s   8 its peak   9 (several) acquisitions
   10 15% / fifteen per cent

Writing

Skills

1 1 victim   2 comprising   3 escalation   4 professional
   5 flagged   6 try   7 troubles   8 watchfulness   9 tendencies
   10 uncover   11 incidents   12 maintained

2 *Suggested answer*

The most recent edition of the KPMG Forensic Fraud Barometer shows that over £1bn in fraud claims were made in the UK courts in 2007, representing the highest amount since 1995. The main victims of fraudulent crimes were identified as government bodies and agencies, which made up £889m of the total. One of the partners of the KPMG forensic team, Hitesh Patel, in an interview with the *Daily Telegraph*, commented that gangs had stepped up their activities, resulting in an escalation of crimes such as VAT frauds, ID thefts and other forms of professional crime. He also added that, in the current economic climate, there is a possibility that other employees may try to solve their financial woes by turning to fraud. Companies should be increasingly cautious of any unusual trends in their accounts, which may help them to discover fraudulent transactions. Last year, £655m of over £1bn in fraudulent crimes took place in London, which means that the capital still maintains the lead in the amount of fraud committed, followed by the Midlands (£117m) and the North-West (£200m).

Exam focus

1 *Suggested answer*

The charges

The accused was charged with one count of fraudulent trading contrary to Section 458 of the Companies Act 1985.

Initial assessment

At a preliminary meeting with the solicitors, a review of the documentation and initial assessment of the charges was carried out. Following this meeting, our assessment letter providing details of our estimated fee for the initial report was prepared.

Initial report

The purpose of this initial report was to identify areas of investigation and evidence for the client's defence in order to carry out the main forensic accounting exercise for the interim report. The initial report was based on 127 pages of witness statements and 669 pages of exhibits. The cost of preparing this report was £5,800 plus VAT.

Interim report

This report identified that extensive forensic accountancy work would be required besides that outlined in the initial report. The interim report was based on defence statements provided by the defendant and witnesses and 33 lever-arch files of records. It was also established that, in addition to the interim report, a final report will be required. The estimated costs of reports is £25,625 and £15,000 plus VAT. At this stage, funding for the final report has not yet been approved. Consequently, no further work has been undertaken on the case.

2 *Suggested answer*

This survey is based on questionnaires regarding the type of fraud and fraudsters, which were completed by the top management of 100 medium-sized private companies. The results show that 25% of fraudsters in companies were employed in mid-management. In addition, the survey indicates that the profile of a typical fraudster is male, between 31 and 40 years old and has been working in the firm for at least five years. Most respondents stated that the majority of cases of fraud were not publicized. Generally, the culprits were merely asked to leave and did so immediately.

The findings of the survey regarding the management's attitude to the prevention of fraud indicate that many managers believe the most effective ways of tackling fraud are preventative, namely with improved fraud risk management and stricter controls.

In addition to serious cases of fraud, respondents answered questions regarding incidents of petty fraud. The majority of managers reported that funds lost in this way were usually recovered. Finally, 80% of managers believed that implementing a procedure of whistle-blowing enabled companies to curb the number of fraudulent activities.

(180 words)

8 Banking

Reading

Skills

1 1 c 2 e 3 j 4 l 5 d 6 h 7 i 8 f 9 m 10 k 11 g 12 a

2 1 … increased accountability and transparency.

  2 … part of the government.

  3 … scrutinized.

  4 … their freedom is constantly constrained by politicians.

  5 … account for their actions and show shareholders that they are operating efficiently / effectively.

3 1 D 2 F 3 A 4 H 5 B 6 I 7 G 8 E 9 C

Exam focus

1 1 g 2 f 3 a 4 k 5 d 6 l 7 b 8 e 9 c 10 m 11 h 12 j

2 1 maintenance 2 regulatory 3 jeopardy 4 bankruptcies 5 authorization 6 security

3 1 D 2 A 3 E 4 B 5 G 6 F

Phrase C is not used.

Listening

1 *Suggested answers*

  1 Banks have lent too much to people who cannot repay and are short of funds.

  2 It means that their balance sheets will be have to be scrutinized more carefully.

  3 The Financial Reporting Council (FRC), which also regulates the audit industry.

2 1 to hide 2 careful 3 accounts 4 written off 5 extra funds 6 balance sheets 7 rescue package 8 regulating 9 risks 10 diligence

Exam focus

2 1 for Central Banks 2 straightforward, expert analysis 3 banking professionals 4 numerous accounting rules 5 valuable practice aids 6 bank's financial position 7 applicable to banks 8 Leading international experts 9 standard-setting 10 goldmine (of information)

4

Topic		Statement
Speaker 1	Movement towards fair-value accounting	B
Speaker 2	New regulations and requirements	A
Speaker 3	Obstacles facing graduate accountancy professionals	C

Speaking

Skills

1 1 activities 2 laws 3 regulations 4 aim 5 depositors 6 licence 7 criteria 8 tests 9 management 10 concern 11 capital 12 debts

Writing

Skills

1 1 of 2 the 3 by 4 the 5 with 6 to 7 in 8 for 9 a 10 with 11 to 12 on

Exam focus

1 *Suggested answer*

Results of the survey indicate that while 83% of respondents understand what is meant by the term 'carbon footprint', 17% stated that they did not.

The survey also revealed that 55% of respondents have not yet made any attempts to reduce the carbon footprint of the company. On the other hand, 45% said that they had implemented some steps to minimize their carbon footprint. In answer to the question 'How important is businesses' role in reducing the impact of climate change?', over half of those who took part in the survey ranked this factor 'very important', 33% said it was 'quite important', and a further 7% responded 'not very important'. Only a small minority of respondees – 3% – considered this factor to be 'not at all important'.

In response to question 4 on the questionnaire, many respondents (45% 'quite important') believed that customers or clients attached some importance to environmental issues, while 42% stated that it was 'not very important' and 4% 'not at all important'. In contrast, only 9% of those interviewed believed that this issue was 'very important'.

Finally, the survey revealed that a startling 70% of those who took part were in favour of the government enforcing measures to make businesses adopt more environmentally friendly processes, and 30% opposed this move.

(213 words)

2 *Suggested answer*

Report

Subject: Expansion plans

Regarding the company's expansion plans and the application for a loan facility to purchase new bottling equipment, the application should be accompanied by the last three years' management records, as well as the financial statements. Before considering the loan application, the bank will require a more complete picture of performance. They will also expect a cashflow statement, along with a list of assets and liabilities. In addition to the said documents, an executive summary should be compiled. This should outline the amount and type of loan applied for, state the purpose of the loan and how it will be repaid. It will also be useful to provide the projections for production in the factory after the new equipment has been installed.

The company's accounts over the past three years reveal steady financial performance with a remarkable level of growth. The high increase in sales over the last two years and the number of wholesale orders, including recent contracts to supply the Asda chain of supermarkets, underlines the need for an increase in production.

All the above-mentioned factors, combined with the company's history of excellent cash management, as well as the capacity of the factory to triple production after expansion, should, in my opinion, put the company in a strong position to take on a loan, and the bank should be happy to provide the loan in such circumstances.

(232 words)

9 Insurance

Reading
Skills
1 1 e 2 f 3 k 4 b 5 a 6 l 7 d 8 g 9 c 10 j 11 h 12 i
2 1 insurance 2 loss 3 confidence 4 disclose 5 concealed
   6 judge 7 risk 8 premium
3 1 F 2 B 3 G 4 C 5 A 6 D
   Paragraph E is not used.

Exam focus
1 1 establish 2 undertakings 3 specific 4 format 5 disclosure
   6 based 7 conventions 8 practice(s)
2 1 Title: A
      1 F 2 D 3 E
   2 Title: C
      1 E 2 F 3 D

Listening
Skills
1 Suggested answers
   1 'Fair value' is used as an estimate of the market value of an asset (or liability) for which a market price cannot be determined.
   2 Supervision of the insurance sector is important to ensure compliance with licensing and prudential requirements, to evaluate the financial condition of insurance providers, and to take action where the requirements are breached or an insurer's soundness is at risk.
2 Sentences 1, 4 and 6 are true.
3 1 I want to argue … in my view
   4 I tend to think … I am totally convinced
   6 I feel
4 1 He was working for a larger, national accounting firm.
   2 That they were not being served by the company's business model.
   3 They negotiated a friendly buyout with their employer and established Strohm Ballweg LLP in Madison.
   4 They now have three partners, 15 employees and more than 75 clients.
   5 They decided to focus on providing accounting services to the insurance industry.
   6 Auditing and tax services, regulatory filing and other back-office services.

Exam focus
1 Suggested answers
   1 be unclear 2 increased 3 affecting the whole part
   4 a method used by insurance companies to reduce their exposure to sudden and severe losses caused by catastrophic events 5 lively discussions 6 firmly established and difficult to change
2 1 greater supervision 2 transfer of risk 3 financially sound
   4 reporting requirements 5 guarantee fund
   6 general insurance business 7 Treasury 8 (full) responsibility

Speaking
Skills
2 1 b 2 c 3 a 4 b 5 b 6 b 7 c 8 a 9 a

Writing
Skills
1 1 e 2 f 3 b 4 c 5 h 6 j 7 a 8 d 9 i 10 g
2 Suggested answer
   I am writing in response to your advertisement for a forensic accountant. I am a qualified Chartered Accountant and loss adjuster with over 15 years' experience in chartered accountancy and loss adjustment.

   For the past five years, I have specialized in business and credit loss. One of my recent assignments involved a business interruption claim for a leading global logistics firm after its warehouse facilities and goods to the value of £2 million were destroyed by fire. I also worked closely with Emerald Pharmaceuticals to investigate their loss of surgical equipment resulting from an explosion. Moreover, I handled a substantial advance loss-of-profit claim for a major oil company for damage to its refinery during construction.

   Other relevant experience in the field of forensic accounting includes leading a loss-adjustment investigation for a global credit insurer.

   In the light of my extensive experience in the field, I am convinced that I am a highly suitable candidate for the position advertised and would make an invaluable contribution to any forensic accounting team.

   I look forward to your reply.

   (175 words)

Exam focus
1 1 In particular 2 In accordance with 3 In consequence
   4 For this reason 5 Notwithstanding 6 In addition
2 ~~The~~ research by **the** Association of British Insurers has shown that ~~the~~ UK insurance companies have paid up £5.5bn in ~~the~~ tax to the government. The group's members paid £3.1bn in ~~a~~ taxes for 2006–2007, ranking it as **the** third-highest amount of corporation tax of any sector. Besides ~~the~~ corporation tax, insurance providers collected **an** additional £3.4bn in tax on behalf of **the** government through taxes such as ~~the~~ PAYE, employee National Insurance (NI) and Insurance Premium Tax (IPT). **The** data is the first-ever breakdown of **the** insurance industry's contribution to the Treasury. It takes into account all direct and indirect taxes, as well as ~~an~~ employment and environment taxes. **A** spokesman from **the** ABI commented that these results highlighted **the** success of the industry.

10 Bankruptcy

Reading

Skills

1 1 c 2 d 3 a 4 g 5 h 6 j 7 e 8 b 9 f 10 i

2 1 Vice President of Internal Audit
   2 *Extraordinary Circumstances: The Journey of a Corporate Whistleblower*
   3 $11 billion

5 1 C 2 A 3 F 4 E 5 B
   Sentence D does not fit.

Exam focus

2 1 limits 2 possession 3 supervision 4 fiduciary 5 appointed
   6 straight bankruptcy 7 property 8 converts 9 majority
   10 purposes 11 wiping out

3 1 G 2 E 3 D 4 A 5 B 6 C
   Sentence F does not fit.

Listening

Skills

1 1 h 2 a 3 d 4 c 5 f 6 b 7 e 8 g

2 1 A 2 C 3 B 4 A

3 1 He was the court-appointed examiner.
   2 In Manhattan, in the summer of 2002.
   3 There were massive accounting irregularities.
   4 It has become a kind of 'poster child' for corporate governance failures this century.
   5 He will only cover the results of the completed investigations which have been made public.

4 1 in a bankruptcy 2 an independent investigation
   3 establish what happened 4 potential courses
   5 Department of Justice 6 creditors

Exam focus

2 Speaker 1: D, E, I Speaker 2: B, H, J Speaker 3: F, K
   Speaker 4: C Speaker 5: A
   Topic G is not mentioned.

Writing

Skills

1 1 H 2 G 3 J 4 I 5 C 6 E 7 A 8 F 9 D 10 B

2 1 allegations 2 governance 3 proceedings 4 illegalities
   5 fraudulent 6 irregularities 7 appointment 8 guidance
   9 failure 10 recommendation

Exam focus

1 *Suggested answer*

Dear Mr Aziz,

Thank you for your recent letter.

Certainly, my client achieved remarkable results last year, considering the subdued DIY market. This growth is mainly due to the Regal product range, introduced 18 months ago, which has been very popular with consumers and has caused profits to rise significantly.

As you mentioned in your letter, building estimates for the warehouse were higher than the original figure, as the architect submitted plans for a slightly larger building to accommodate the Regal show kitchens. This range continues to be the market leader, hence the extra cost is expected to be covered by increased profits. The increase in contractors' fees is due to the demand for installation services, which are also expected to bring in extra income.

Regarding your query about the projected figures, although I appreciate that competition in the DIY market is tough, my client now has an exclusive contract with a major hotel chain to provide the Regal bathroom range. This contract will also contribute to the increase in market share, as extensive market research has shown.

Yours sincerely,

(180 words)

2 *Suggested answer*

Report

Subject: Company Voluntary Arrangement

A Company Voluntary Arrangement (CVA) is an insolvency procedure that allows a financially troubled company to reach agreement with its creditors about payment of its debts over an agreed period of time. It is important to note that a CVA can only be proposed if a company is insolvent or contingently insolvent.

Should you decide to take this way forward, setting up a CVA can be proposed by the directors of the company, the administrators of the company, or the liquidator of the company. When the CVA has been proposed, the nominee reports to the court to arrange a meeting of creditors and shareholders to consider the proposal. At this meeting, the creditors vote. If the majority of creditors at the meeting, representing 75% of the debt, vote in favour, the CVA is approved.

In terms of the advantages of a CVA, the most significant of these is that the company is able to continue trading during the CVA and afterwards. In addition, the reputation of the business is not adversely affected, as there is no stigma linked to a CVA compared to going into liquidation.

Our firm has considerable experience in handling insolvency cases, and I myself am an insolvency practitioner, so we would be able to assist you with the CVA process. However, at this stage, it is important that you consider all the options for solving the short-term cashflow problems that the company has been facing before making this decision.

(248 words)